INTERNATIONAL SANCTIONS IN
CONTEMPORARY PERSPECTIVE

Also by Margaret P. Doxey

ECONOMIC SANCTIONS AND INTERNATIONAL
ENFORCEMENT

International Sanctions in Contemporary Perspective

Margaret P. Doxey

Professor of Political Studies
Trent University, Canada

St. Martin's Press   New York

First published in the United States of America in 1987

Printed in Hong Kong

ISBN   0–312–00758–2

Library of Congress Cataloging-in-Publication Data
Doxey, Margaret P.
International sanctions in contemporary perspective.
Bibliography: p.
Includes index.
1. Sanctions (International law)   2. Economic
sanctions.   I. Title.
JX1246.D69   1987   341.5′8   87–4344
ISBN   0–312–00758–2

Contents

Preface

This book presents a new analysis of international sanctions. Its object is to provide a balanced picture of recent and contemporary state practice, to elucidate problems of sanctions application and impact, and to review major policy considerations which are relevant to official sanctioning decisions. The frequency with which governments now find themselves confronting such decisions underlines the importance of the subject for practitioners as well as for scholars.

The book takes account not only of sanctions imposed within institutional frameworks, such as United Nations sanctions against Rhodesia (Zimbabwe) and Organisation of American States action against Cuba, but also of group responses to international wrong-doing which have been organised on a voluntary, *ad hoc* basis. In the 1980s Iran, the Soviet Union, Poland, Argentina and Libya have experienced penalties of this kind. South Africa receives particular attention as a potential target of comprehensive international sanctions.

The scope of the study is therefore wider than that of my earlier work *Economic Sanctions and International Enforcement* (Macmillan for the Royal Institute of International Affairs, 2nd edn, 1980), although where appropriate I have drawn on case material and developed arguments first presented there.

In writing the book I have benefited greatly from many formal and informal exchanges of views with colleagues and friends in academic and government circles in Canada, Britain and the United States. It would be invidious to name some and impossible to name them all. In Canada, however, I owe a special debt to fellow-participants in a continuing colloquium on international institutions sponsored by the Centre for International Studies at the University of Toronto and supported by a grant from the Donner Foundation. The meetings of this group, expertly led by Professors John Holmes and Robert Spencer, have provided intellectual stimulation and numerous opportunities for informed and lively debate. In 1982–3 I spent two terms as Academic Visitor with the Department of International Relations at the London School of Economics and this, too, helped in developing new perspectives on familiar issues. It should also be recorded that the typology of non-violent sanctions at the end of Chapter 1, and some of the discussion of goals of states imposing sanctions in Chapter 7, were first presented at an inter-disciplinary conference on North–South relations organised by the Department of International Politics, the University College of Wales, Aberystwyth, in July 1984 and subsequently incorporated in Chapter 5 of Moorhead Wright (ed.) *Rights and Obligations in North–South Relations: Ethical Dimensions of Global Problems* (London, Macmillan; New York, St. Martin's Press, 1986).

I am grateful to Trent University for research support and to the librarians and staff at the Canadian Institute of International Affairs and Chatham House who have given invaluable and gracious assistance. And no words can express my debt to Carol Wood whose superb secretarial skills and friendly interest in my work have contributed in no small measure to the completion of this book.

Trent University   Margaret P. Doxey
Ontario
April 1986

Afterword

In the six months that have elapsed since this book was finished, there have been important developments in respect of sanctions against South Africa, where the government of President Botha has shown no disposition to discuss meaningful power-sharing with leaders of the black community. Instead it imposed harsher measures to crush opposition and launched armed attacks against neighbouring states, accusing them of harbouring 'bases' for the African National Congress. The reaction of all anti-apartheid groups was to call even more urgently for international sanctions and their position was endorsed by the Report of the Commonwealth Eminent Persons Group (*Mission to South Africa*, published by Penguin Books for the Commonwealth Secretariat, June 1986) which noted with disappointment that the South African government had shown 'no genuine intention . . . to dismantle apartheid' (p. 137). According to this Group, the question for Commonwealth governments was not whether sanctions would 'compel change; it is already the case that their absence and Pretoria's belief that they need not be feared, defers change', but the need for concerted action (p. 140).

In August a mini-summit of seven Commonwealth Heads of Government brought further confirmation of the sharp division of opinion between Britain and the rest of the membership on the sanctions issue. The leaders of Australia, Bahamas, Canada, India and Zimbabwe agreed to impose new restrictions on their countries' dealings with South Africa and to urge all other Commonwealth governments to follow suit. These sanctions include a ban on air links with South Africa; a ban on new investment, bank loans to the public and private sector and reinvestment of profits in South Africa; the prohibition of imports of coal, iron and steel, uranium and agricultural products from South Africa; and the termination of double taxation agreements. For its part, in spite of intense intra-Commonwealth pressure exerted throughout June and July which suggested that the viability of the whole association might be at stake, the British government limited its action to a voluntary ban on new investment and on tourism in South Africa, and a commitment to ban imports from South Africa of coal, iron and steel and gold coins if its European Community partners would do likewise. In September, the EC Foreign Ministers agreed to ban imports of iron and steel, but not coal, and Japan, too, embargoed the import of South African iron and steel and withdrew visas for South African tourists.

These has also been a major shift in US policy towards South Africa as a result of the override by the Congress on 3 October of President Reagan's veto of sanctions legislation previously passed by both houses. As a result, the United States now bans all new investment and bank loans in South Africa; prohibits the import of South African coal, iron and steel, uranium, textiles, agricultural produce and food; and denies landing rights to South African airlines. Like the British Prime Minister, President Reagan still maintains that sanctions will do more harm than good.

Although there is some overlap among Commonwealth, EC and US measures, they form an unco-ordinated patchwork of restrictions which will take effect at different times. They will not cripple the South African economy; nor will they carry a high cost for those imposing them. Important minerals such as platinum and chrome are not included in any of the embargoes. No doubt there will be some negative effect on South African industry and agriculture, but it was stated openly in the US Senate debates that the main objective of the sanctions was to demonstrate not only to blacks and whites in South Africa but to the whole world that the United States will act to uphold human dignity and racial equality. Similar statements have been made by Commonwealth and European governments and there can be no doubt that the intent of this latest round of sanctions is pre-eminently symbolic. Nevertheless, the measures are not inconsequential. They increase the cost of intransigence for the South African government, which must also ponder whether international momentum will continue to build for even more stringent and comprehensive measures and whether, in spite of the considerable defensive strengths it can muster, black South Africans will now be encouraged to press even harder for radical change. The sanctions increase psychological pressure on South African whites, increasing their isolation from the international community.

The reaction of the South African government to these new developments is not yet known, although it has threatened counter-measures, but it must surely be the hope of all who wish to avert further violence in South Africa that the sanctions now in place not only carry a clear message of repudiation of apartheid and support for human rights, but also make a positive contribution to a democratic and peaceful outcome.

1 The Scope of the Study

Over the past decade, international sanctions have featured prominently in state practice. Not surprisingly they have also received considerable attention in the news media, in public debate and in scholarly writing.[1] A series of high-profile cases of sanctioning outside the United Nations framework began in late 1979 with the response to the Tehran hostages crisis and the Soviet intervention in Afghanistan; sanctions were also imposed following the introduction of martial law in Poland in 1981, in the Falklands war in 1982, and against Libya in 1986. In all of these cases, with the exception of the Falklands war, the United States was the initiator and main proponent of collective measures. Sanctions ordered by the UN Security Council on Rhodesia (now Zimbabwe) were formally lifted in December 1979 in the wake of a settlement providing for full independence with majority rule, but discussion and debate continued with intermittent vigour in the UN and other international forums on the pros and cons of applying economic sanctions to South Africa. The institutionalised system of racial discrimination (apartheid) which denies political rights to South African blacks, as well as South Africa's continued administration of Namibia in defiance of UN and World Court rulings, provide moral and legal grounds for sanctions in this case. A mandatory embargo on arms sales to South Africa was imposed by the Security Council in 1977 and in 1985 unprecedented and sustained levels of internal unrest in South African black townships, accompanied by renewed repression by the authorities, brought widespread calls for stronger measures to which western governments proved more responsive than in the past. In July the Security Council encouraged UN members to adopt voluntary sanctions and in September the United States, European Community members and other western governments took some action on this recommendation. In October Commonwealth Heads of Government meeting in the Bahamas agreed on a set of mild penalties with a commitment to review the situation in six months' time. In the long run it is not impossible that

1

mandatory economic sanctions may be imposed against South Africa.

Recent experience with international sanctions and the continuing controversy over South Africa make a new and comprehensive study of the subject both timely and useful. It is hoped that analysis of the motives and intentions of governments applying sanctions, assessment of the difficulties of constructing a genuine multilateral effort, and consideration of the effects of sanctions both on the target and on third states will provide a clearer understanding of an important area of statecraft.

At the outset it is important to clarify what is meant by the term 'international sanction' in this study, particularly as current usage reflects a great deal of confusion. Part of the difficulty is that international society is decentralised and anarchical, possessing none of the law-making and law-enforcement mechanisms which are associated with sanctions and sanctioning procedures within the nation–state. Analogies between the domestic and international scene can therefore be misleading. And problems in both theory and practice of international sanctions are compounded by the very limited relevance of international institutions for the process of dispute settlement and the growing tendency for states to take punitive retaliatory action outside organisational frameworks.

For lawyers, negative sanctions are measures of enforcement which follow violations of law. They are penalties which indicate the limits of permissible conduct and encourage compliance with known rules. Ideally they should deter wrong-doers by the prospect of punishment, but if some are not deterred, imposing sanctions can perhaps deter them from repeating their misdeeds as well as serving as a warning to others. There is no problem with this concept of sanctions within national societies and where designated authorities make and enforce law, the sanctions label can be applied to penalties for law-breaking irrespective of the legitimacy of the regime and the character of the laws it enacts and enforces. But international society is altogether different. The prime actors are not individuals or corporations but sovereign states, subject to no over-arching authority, and there are no international institutional structures or institutionalised procedures comparable to those found within states. The concept of sanctions described above is therefore not applicable without qualification at the international level. Even if a broader definition of sanctions is adopted which encompasses measures defending conformity with custom as well as with law, there is still the problem that the international milieu does not exhibit social cohesion to any marked degree. It is thus not surprising that for laymen, journalists and many scholars, international sanctions no longer have specific legal connotations and that a variety of meanings are in vogue.

David Baldwin confronts this problem in his recent monograph *Economic Statecraft*, noting three common meanings of the term 'economic sanctions': the first 'a rather narrow concept referring to the use of economic measures to enforce international law'; the second 'refers to the types of values ... intended to be reduced or augmented in the target state'; the third 'corresponds to the concept of economic techniques of statecraft' which form the subject of his book.[2] These techniques are defined as 'governmental influence attempts relying primarily on resources that have a reasonable semblance of a market price in terms of money'.[3]

The second meaning of economic sanctions is specifically effect-oriented[4] and need not concern us here except in so far as it raises the interesting possibility of positive sanctions (rewards and inducements) as well as the more familiar negative sanctions,[5] but the first and third bear closer examination. Baldwin contrasts them in terms of scope: economic sanctions can be economic measures used to enforce international law, a meaning he characterises as 'narrowly legalistic and therefore unsuitable for general foreign policy analysis';[6] alternatively they mean governmental influence attempts which rely on economic instrumentalities. But the broad scope of this third meaning effectively drains the term 'sanction' of content by allowing it to describe any or all politically-motivated injurious or coercive acts of foreign economic policy.[7] By analogy, diplomatic, cultural or military sanctions would also mean governmental influence attempts, albeit using different techniques. While one sympathises with Baldwin's comment that 'the term economic sanctions is used in so many different ways that there is much to be said for avoiding it altogether',[8] it is preferable for international relations scholars to make an effort to salvage some meaning for international sanctions, not only because the term *economic* sanctions 'is so deeply embedded in the literature of economic statecraft that ignoring it is impossible',[9] but because sanctions of all kinds feature prominently in governmental pronouncements and practice.

No doubt in the 1930s things seemed more straightforward. In line with the concept of enforcement of international law, international sanctions meant League of Nations sanctions; in other words, penalties to be collectively imposed by members of the body responsible for international peace and security on those who violated their obligations under the League Covenant. This concept of penalties in an international framework was carried forward in the United Nations Charter which introduced new norms of human rights and also gave limited authority to regional bodies to act in defence of regional peace and security. Until quite recently the major cases of sanctions which attracted scholars' attention were those sponsored by the League, the UN, and regional bodies, particularly the Organisation of American States (OAS). Unilateral acts of retaliation[10] were not usually referred to as sanctions; nor was economic warfare so described, whether employed in a 'hot' or 'cold' war. For instance, western strategic embargoes against the Soviet Union, in place since the late 1940s, were not described by scholars or practitioners as 'sanctions'.

But the moral claims of competing ideologies, particularly those reflected in East–West rivalry, have encouraged widespread official use of the term sanction to invest foreign policy actions with an aura of righteousness. Moreover the trend to adopt collective measures outside the United Nations and other organisational frameworks has inevitably extended the scope of sanctioning. It would now be unrealistic to limit the international sanctions label to UN enforcement measures, or to measures imposed by any international body against its own members. But it is still possible – and desirable – to preserve the sense of sanctions as penalties linked to real or alleged misconduct. From this perspective, violations of international law and/or the use of institutionally-based enforcement mechanisms are possible but not essential components of sanctioning. What is important is to distinguish sanctions from violent or non-violent techniques employed specifically to further the interests of one or more states at the expense of others. International sanctions, as investigated in this study, are penalties threatened or imposed as a declared consequence of the target's failure to observe international standards or international obligations.

What these standards and obligations are, to what extent states are legally or morally bound by them, and the appropriateness of a sanctions response are questions to be explored in this and subsequent chapters.

The definition of international sanctions adopted here is unlikely to satisfy everyone. It will be too broad for some and too narrow for others and is inevitably surrounded by controversial 'grey areas'. But it preserves the meaning of a sanction as a modality for defending standards of behaviour, is compatible with contemporary practice, and sets some boundaries to the inquiry by differentiating between sanctions as a response to unacceptable conduct in the context of agreed norms and other forms of interstate pressure.[11] From an analytical viewpoint, consideration of the validity of a 'sanctions' label can itself be enlightening. Certain forms of foreign policy behaviour are excluded; among them would be coercive acts of an economic nature which are designed to secure advantages for the coercing state(s). Such acts are condemned in the Declaration on Principles of International Law concerning Friendly Relations and Cooperation among States (General Assembly Resolution 2625 (xxv)) and might themselves give cause for sanctions. Economic warfare, whether supplementing force in a 'hot' war or used alone in a 'cold' war should also be distinguished from sanctioning when its object is to improve the relative position or chances of 'winning' for the state(s) employing these tactics. As noted earlier, western strategic embargoes were not described as sanctions, nor should they have been; similarly, Arab League boycotts of Israel and Israel's allies and trading partners are not sanctions and have not been so labelled.[12]

The umbrella-nature of this definition of international sanctions as international penalties allows for, and indeed requires, elaboration in terms of the norm(s) they purport to defend, the sponsorship the sanctions enjoy and the nature of the measures themselves. International sanctions may be adopted inside or outside institutional frameworks: if the former, they may be mandatory or voluntary; if the latter, they can only be voluntary. Except incidentally, unilateral measures which could qualify as sanctions in terms of our definition are not considered in this study which focuses on sanctions adopted by groups of states. It should be noted that unilateral sanctions can either be acts of self-help directly and specifically related to an injury sustained by the state imposing them (retorsion or reprisal in legal parlance), or penalties for violations of internationally-accepted rules or standards which reflect general or group interests. Claims to be defending general or group values, whether or not national interests are also involved, carry more conviction if a number of states are willing to adopt sanctions against the offender.[13] As discussed later in this book, motives for action are often very hard to determine with accuracy, but the tests of injury and/or advantage to the state resorting to unilateral measures on the one hand, and of clear violation of international standards on the other, can give some indication of the extent to which policy is self-serving. There was, for instance, no question of retaliation for injury to the United States or of advancing its particular interests when the Carter Administration imposed a ban on trade with Uganda in October 1978. The gross and persistent violations of human rights perpetrated by Idi Amin had shocked world public opinion and (eventually) produced verbal condemnation by Commonwealth Heads of Government, but there was no call for sanctions by African governments in the Organisation of African Unity or at the UN.[14] The US action, which (deplorably) remained unilateral, was obviously grounded in humanitarian concerns. In other cases both particular and general interests may be served. For instance, the British government had a constitutional right to respond to the illegal declaration of independence by the Smith regime in Rhodesia in 1965, but there was also concern for the rights of Rhodesian blacks, while in the Tehran hostages case, there was direct injury to US interests as well as a breach of general international law.

In UN forums the question whether a situation merits the imposition of sanctions may be hotly disputed and there is scope for widely differing interpretations of universal norms. The veto protects permanent members of the Security Council and their friends and clients from any possibility of mandatory UN sanctions. And the absence of an effective UN enforcement system gives ample opportunity for governments in other institutional settings to debate what rules exist; whether they have been flouted; whether penalties should be imposed; what form they should take. As noted above, one of the reasons for the increasingly common use of the term 'sanction' is the preference of governments to assert ethical grounds for their foreign policy behaviour. They will say that they are imposing 'sanctions' because this suggests the defence of legitimate, worthy and general interests rather than the advance of particular and self-serving interests of their own. But before accepting these claims at face value, the analyst must assess the circumstances of each case. Have rules or principles been violated? What is the authority or justification of those imposing sanctions to take retaliatory action? What are they really up to? And there is no doubt that as state practice in sanctioning moves further away from institutional frameworks, uncertainties multiply.

Besides the possibly questionable legitimacy of the norm, and of the group claiming to defend it, a further set of problems relates to the measures themselves. Standardised penalties for designated offences do not exist at the international level and governments resorting to sanctions have a very wide range of choice. In conventional parlance, sanctions usually mean non-violent measures, particularly economic measures, and this reflects state practice, but the possible use of military measures as sanctions deserves mention. Such measures of enforcement did not feature in the League Covenant and cannot be ordered by the Security Council under Chapter vii of the Charter because agreements under Article 43 making forces available were never concluded. It is also extremely unlikely, although hypothetically not impossible, that the Council would again recommend the use of force as happened in the Korean crisis. Given its role as a body promoting peace, resort to armed force does not seem an appropriate UN response, particularly in an age of nuclear weapons. Without Security Council authorization, force is only permitted to UN members for individual or collective self-defence against armed attack and governments typically justify military action in those terms. Where no case can possibly be made for self-defence, assistance to governments in need of help, or humanitarian concerns have been used as justification.[15] Difficulties in justifying the use of force are illustrated by the claim of the Kennedy Administration that the naval blockade ('quarantine') of Cuba during the missile crisis was a regional response to a threat to the peace of the hemisphere, but was not 'enforcement' because it was voluntary under the Rio Treaty.[16] In regional settings there are obviously 'grey areas'.

The legality and/or appropriateness of non-violent measures

can also be controversial. It has been contended, particularly by governments of developing countries, that economic coercion must also be considered as 'force', outlawed by Article 2 (4) of the UN Charter.[17] Even if one rejects this extreme view, questions can be asked about a government's right to break economic or financial arrangements which have been established by international treaty, particularly if it has suffered no direct injury. In the Falklands conflict, for instance, Argentina challenged the legality of European Community (EC) trade sanctions against it in terms of General Agreement on Tariffs and Trade (GATT) rules, contending that Britain alone, not its EC partners, could allege injury.[18] The proportionality of a response to international rule breaking can also be disputed.

UN sanctions ordered by a Security Council Resolution with at least nine affirmative votes and no veto by a permanent member are unquestionably obligatory for members, although their appropriateness could still be challenged by the offending state and by states which voted against them on the Council (or would have done so if they had had seats there). But mandatory UN sanctions are extremely rare and in other cases individual governments may either apply sanctions which are within their legal competence without violating any international agreements, or they may decide that the illegal policies of the offending state 'legalise' a policy of unilateral or collective retaliation. The absence of any impartial judge of state behaviour and state response allows very thin claims to legality and proportionality to go unchallenged.

This study is principally concerned with non-violent sanctions which include diplomatic and political moves and cultural and communication measures, as well as the broad range of economic measures of a commercial, financial or technological nature. There are also penalties specifically related to membership of international organisations. A full list is provided at the end of this chapter. Preference is often expressed for economic measures because they are seen on the one hand as a non-lethal means of exerting pressure and, on the other, as likely to have some significant impact on the target. Economic sanctions, as distinct from diplomatic and cultural sanctions, are expected to have coercive, as well as demonstrative and punitive effects; in other words the reduction in economic welfare which they inflict should produce psychological and political results. Both major experiments with international sanctions – League of Nations sanctions against Italy in 1935–6 and United Nations sanctions against Rhodesia from 1966–79 – relied heavily on economic measures, as have the sanctioning cases of the past decade. Economic pressure is also advocated as the appropriate means of bringing pressure to bear on the South African government to abandon apartheid. But it cannot be taken for granted that economic sanctions are always the best choice; in fact, scepticism about their efficacy and concern over their drawbacks are widespread. Given that they are seen to bring slow and limited results, and are costly for those imposing them, a decline in usage might have been expected. One of the many questions to be addressed in subsequent chapters is why this has not happened, but the point can be made here that a more sophisticated understanding of the implications of using economic pressure to induce changes in a target's political behaviour has been accompanied by a clearer grasp of the variety of purposes sanctions may really be intended to serve. As far as the ostensible target is concerned, coercion or punishment may be the prime objective, although symbolic condemnation can also be intended. But the ostensible target is not necessarily the only, or even the principal receptor; sanctions may be 'signals' to the domestic constituency of the government(s) imposing them as well as to third states. And for these audiences symbolic and demonstrative functions are the most important.

It should be emphasised that the focus in this study is on sanctions sponsored by governments against other governments and not on unofficial boycotts by consumers or other interest groups, although these can certainly be an important source of pressure in persuading governments to impose sanctions as well as on the targets from whom policy change is desired.[19] To assist in developing answers to questions when and how official international sanctions are imposed and why particular measures are selected or rejected, and to analyse the problems which sanctions bring in their wake, the study begins with a discussion of the authoritative basis for sanctioning in Chapter 2. It proceeds to consider sanctions in practice. Chapters 3 and 4 deal with sanctions imposed by the League and the United Nations while Chapter 5 considers sanctions in regional settings: Eastern Europe, the Western hemisphere and the Arab world. Chapter 6 considers four recent cases where such organisational backing was lacking: the Tehran hostages crisis; Soviet intervention in Afghanistan; the imposition of martial law in Poland; the Falklands war. Drawing on this material for illustration, Chapters 7 and 8 address the problems faced by governments in attempting to orchestrate a collective sanctions programme and consider the impact of such programmes on targets and on third states. It will be clear that an *ad hoc*, non-authorised sanctions effort presents an extremely daunting and complex set of choices for governments. Not only is there no obligation to participate, but the reasons for doing so may have varying degrees of cogency. Ironically, recent experience in the western alliance illustrates that among these reasons intra-group 'penalties' for non-participation levied by more enthusiastic sanctioners may feature quite prominently.

Chapter 9 gives special attention to the case of South Africa which presents difficult choices for western governments, while the final Chapter reviews trends in sanctioning and draws some tentative conclusions of a general nature.

A TYPOLOGY OF NON-VIOLENT SANCTIONS

1. Diplomatic and political measures

    a) Protest, censure, condemnation.
    b) Postponement/cancellation of official visits; meetings; negotiations for treaties and agreements.
    c) Reduction/limitation of scale of diplomatic representation:
        (i) status of post
        (ii) number of diplomatic personnel
        (iii) number of consular offices.
    d) Severance of diplomatic relations.
    e) Non-recognition of new governments, new states.

2. Cultural and communications measures

    a) Reduction/cancellation of cultural exchanges: scientific co-operation; educational links; sporting links; entertainment.

b) Ban on tourism to/from target country.
c) Withdrawal of visas for nationals of target.
d) Restriction/cancellation of telephone, cable, postal links.
e) Restriction/suspension/cancellation of landing, overflight privileges.
f) Restriction/suspension/cancellation of water transit, docking, port privileges.
g) Restriction/suspension/cancellation of land transit privileges.

3. Economic measures

A Financial
   a) Reduction/suspension/cancellation of aid: military, food, development, funding of technical assistance.
   b) Reduction/suspension/cancellation of credit facilities at concessionary/market rates.
   c) Freezing/confiscation of bank assets of target government.
   d) Confiscation/expropriation of other assets belonging to the target.
   e) Ban on interest payments.
   f) Ban on other transfer payments.
   g) Refusal to refinance, reschedule debt repayments (interest and principal).
   h) Control/ban on capital movements.

B Commercial and technical
   a) Quotas on imports.
   b) Quotas on exports.
   c) Restrictive import licensing.
   d) Restrictive export licensing.
   e) Limited/total embargo on imports.
   f) Limited/total embargo on exports.
   g) Discriminatory tariff policy (includes denial of most favoured nation status).
   h) Restriction/cancellation/suspension of fishing rights.
   i) Suspension/cancellation of joint projects, industrial ventures.
   j) Cancellation of trade agreements.
   k) Ban on export of technology.
   l) Blacklisting of individuals/firms trading with the target.

    m) Reduction/suspension/cancellation of technical assistance, training programmes.

    n) Ban on insurance services.

4. Measures relating to status in international organisations

A Membership and participation
    a) Vote against admission. (N.B. this may amount to a veto.)
    b) Vote against acceptance of credentials.
    c) Vote for suspension.
    d) Vote for expulsion.

B Benefits
    a) Vote against loans, grants, technical assistance, other benefits.
    b) Vote for removal of headquarters, regional office from target.

2 International Standards and the Authoritative Basis for Sanctions

It was noted in the previous chapter that international sanctions were not a familiar aspect of statecraft until the twentieth century, when two world wars of horrifying dimensions prompted efforts to lay a more secure foundation for peace and world order. The results of these efforts were embodied in the League of Nations and in its successor organisation the United Nations; bodies which were to be purveyors of peace. Both the League and the UN attempted to institutionalise norms of behaviour which would encourage the peaceful settlement of disputes and limit the use of force between states; the UN has gone further in developing extensive welfare functions including specific concerns for human rights.

Under the Covenant, individual members of the League were to decide if its rules had been broken: collective action (sanctions) would follow. Under the Charter, there was to be collective determination of rule-breaking as well as collective action to deal with it. Such action would be in a different category of behaviour from coercive measures adopted by individual states, or, for that matter, by groups of states seeking to further their own interests at the expense of others. Having a legal and moral basis, these measures would be *sanctions*: authorised against designated wrong-doers. As such they would have a superior status to traditional acts of reprisal.[1]

Article 16 of the League Covenant provided for diplomatic and economic sanctions if members decided that prescribed procedures for dispute settlement had not been followed. Such behaviour was deemed 'an act of war against all other Members of the League' who would immediately sever all trade, financial and personal relations with the offender. Article 39 of the UN Charter permits the Security Council to determine the existence of a threat to the peace, breach of the peace or act of aggression and to order members to impose non-military measures.[2] By establishing procedures for sanctions both the Covenant and the Charter sought to operationalise the concept of enforcement of agreed standards of conduct at the international level. League sanctions were intended to deter would-be rule-breakers, or failing that, to bring rapid compliance by their punitive effect. It was thought that economic weapons, wielded collectively, would have a devastating impact on the target.[3] But from the outset members were unhappy about the obligations Article 16 imposed on them and, as described in more detail in the next chapter, League sanctions were only invoked once, following the Italian invasion of Ethiopia in October 1935. They did not succeed in changing Italian policy and by the time they were lifted in July 1936, the conquest of Ethiopia was complete and its annexation by Italy was soon widely recognised. Clearly the 'system' had not worked and the League derived no credit from the episode.

It is worth noting that the Covenant did not place sweeping restrictions on the use of force by states. Articles 12–15 called for prior use of diplomatic or judicial procedures and a delay of three months after the publication of a League Council report or Council decision before states could legally resort to war. In addition, League authority was never universal: the United States failed to join and the Soviet Union did not become a member until 1934, by which time Japan and Germany had left. In 1928 the United States sponsored the Kellogg–Briand Pact (Pact of Paris) in terms of which a very large number of signatories (including Germany and Japan) renounced war as an instrument of national policy. In practice this had no effect. Those who intended to use force in the pursuit of their foreign policy goals went ahead and did so, and indeed the League Covenant offered no mechanisms for the peaceful adjustment of claims of dissatisfied states.

The uneasy combination of the renunciation of war as an instrument of national policy and power-based enforcement was revived in the UN Charter. Once again the victors in a major war set up an institutional framework for the orderly conduct of international relations although this time they all became founding members. A comprehensive ban on the use of force was given a prominent place in the UN Charter. In Article 2 (4) members of the new organisation accepted an obligation to refrain from the use of force in their relations with other states, reserving only the inherent right of self-defence against armed attack until measures had been taken by the UN (Article 51). They accepted binding commitments to carry out Security Council decisions (Article 25); and to seek peaceful resolution of their disputes (Article 33). The Charter also contained pledges by members to uphold and promote human rights within their domestic jurisdictions (Articles 55 and 56) and to promote the advancement of non-self-governing peoples in their colonial empires. This laid the groundwork for developing new standards of human rights, a process carried forward in the Universal Declaration of Human Rights (1948), in subsequent General Assembly Declarations such as those concerning the Granting of Independence to Colonial Countries and Peoples (1960) and the Elimination of All Forms of Racial Discrimination (1963) and in international conventions such as the two Human Rights Covenants (1966).

The UN has therefore developed a much more comprehensive set of international standards to which enforcement measures can be linked; moreover Chapter VII of the Charter gives the Security Council executive authority to categorise dangerous situations and decide on preventive and enforcement measures. Its power to deal with threats to the peace as well as breaches of the peace and acts of aggression allows domestic situations, such as apartheid in South Africa, to be brought under a sanctions order.[4] There is also flexibility in the choice of UN sanctions; in place of the automatic sanctions of Article 16 of the Covenant, Article 41 of the Charter allows diplomatic and economic relations to be completely or partially severed and a variety of other non-violent measures to be selected. Article 5 provides that suspension from UN membership can be effected by the General Assembly on the recommendation of the Security Council if the latter has ordered preventive or enforcement action, while expulsion of a member who has persistently violated Charter principles is possible under Article 6, again through a General Assembly resolution after recommendation by the Security Council.

The text of the Charter might suggest an 'authority model' rather than a 'power model', reflecting in the words of Ian Clark 'orderly procedures and institutionalised behaviour'.[5] But, as Clark notes, this model exists 'mainly in the imagination'.[6]

Neither in 1945, nor at any time since, have UN members shown a general disposition to allow Charter principles and procedures to govern their behaviour. Deep East–West cleavages were apparent from the outset and the term Cold War was soon in widespread use; North–South divisions have characterised the decolonisation and post-decolonisation periods. Ideological, racial, religious, economic and cultural differences, which seem to be increasing rather than diminishing, militate against any universal consensus on values; violent conflict between states and gross violations of human rights within them are commonplace.

One need hardly belabour the point that the UN is no more able to regulate state conduct than any other international organisation unless member states are willing that it should do so. It has no independent authority and no independent resources. Baer's description of the League as 'a structure wherein commonly shared purposes might be translated into common action'[7] is equally valid for the UN. Majority support, and even consensus, has been quite readily obtained in the General Assembly for standard-setting on broad issues of friendly relations, decolonisation and human rights. Voting for such declarations is cost-free and looks good. But UN condemnation of standard-breaking by members has been highly selective and many glaring cases of human rights abuse have gone uncensored. In a recent monograph, Samuel Kim noted 'seven post-holocaust cases of genocide which managed to escape collective sanctions'.[8] The UN's one major comprehensive case of economic sanctions was directed at the white minority regime in Rhodesia (see Chapter 4 below), which was unwise enough to make a unilateral declaration of independence (UDI) in 1965, thus forfeiting British protection. As far as other cases are concerned, the Security Council has either not discussed them at all, or failed to come to a decision because the veto of one or more of the permanent members has been used in defence of their own or their clients' interests. In reality there was never any possibility that the Security Council could develop a consistent pattern of sanctioning. Given the lack of consensus on unacceptable behaviour and the absence of a combined will to respond to wrong-doing, mandatory UN sanctions are predictably unlikely. In consequence, they cannot function effectively as indicators of the limits of permissible conduct or as deterrents to misconduct.

None of the post-1979 cases of group retaliation noted in Chapter 1 had full Security Council backing. Measures were adopted voluntarily by individual governments acting in uneasy concert; in most cases there was disagreement about the kind of response which should be made. Certainly, in the Tehran hostages case norm violation was not in doubt, and in the Falklands crisis Argentina's resort to force was generally deplored, and it is interesting that in both these cases the Security Council did rule on inappropriate behaviour although no sanctions were ordered.[9] The General Assembly condemned the Soviet intervention in Afghanistan (and, later, the United States military action in Grenada), but martial law in Poland was not a matter for Security Council or General Assembly action.

Given the sporadic nature of the UN's sanctioning record, which obviously reflects conflicting interpretations of norms as well as disagreement that they have been violated and/or that penalties are called for, claims of authority for its pronouncements require careful scrutiny. In what circumstances are UN sanctions authoritative?

Maximum legitimation comes with a binding order from the Security Council, even though such orders have been few and far between. The only two examples at the time of writing are general sanctions on Rhodesia post-UDI and the arms embargo imposed on South Africa in 1977. Without a Security Council order there are no mandatory UN sanctions, but the absence of such an order does not remove all possibility of sanctions deriving some international authoritativeness from UN sources. Using practice as a guide, it seems that there may be varying degrees of partial legitimation.

In the first place, a Security Council recommendation that members should voluntarily adopt sanctions gives significant backing to such moves. This development in Security Council practice can be seen in Resolution 569 of 26 July 1985 which by 13 votes to none, with Britain and the United States abstaining, called on the South African government to end the recently-proclaimed state of emergency in that country and encouraged UN members to impose selective cultural and economic sanctions on South Africa. France, which sponsored the resolution, had already recalled its ambassador from Pretoria and banned new investment in South Africa.

Secondly, Security Council condemnation, even if it is not accompanied by sanctions orders or recommendations, may give some moral reinforcement to retaliatory action taken by states who can then claim to be defending universal values as well as their own interests. In this context it is interesting to consider Security Council Resolution 573 of 4 October 1985, adopted by 14:0 with the United States abstaining, which characterised Israel's attack on the headquarters of the Palestine Liberation Organisation in Tunisia as an 'act of armed aggression' and supported Tunisia's 'right to appropriate reparations'. But such moral reinforcement will obviously be less telling if the vote in the Council is close, or if there are a significant number of abstentions. As discussed further in Chapter 6, Britain was pleased to have Resolution 502 passed by the Security Council very early in the Falklands crisis, confirming that a breach of the peace had occurred and calling on Argentina to withdraw its forces from the islands. However, the British government did not seek a sanctions resolution because its certain veto by the USSR was judged as likely to weaken rather than strengthen Britain's position. It is perhaps open to question whether this would have been the case. In the Tehran hostages case, the Soviet Union did veto the draft resolution (S/13735) proposed by the United States which would have imposed sanctions on Iran, but the censure of Iran's behaviour contained in earlier Security Council resolutions and in the World Court's ruling was not affected, and as noted by Michael Reisman, not only President Carter, but also the foreign Ministers of the European Community (EC), cited this vetoed resolution in official statements explaining their imposition of sanctions.[10] Reisman raises the possibility of a trend to 'a new modality of Security Council lawmaking' where a majority vote, irrespective of the veto, could carry 'prescriptive and authorising power' and warns correctly that this could have serious implications for the viability of the UN by further undermining its acceptability to the United States and, no doubt, to other members of the Security Council.[11]

What about General Assembly action? Its powers in respect of peace and security issues are limited to recommendations, which are not binding, but this does not mean they are necessarily devoid of authority. If the Security Council has already pronounced on a dispute or situation, Assembly resolutions are supportive. In other cases, they provide evidence of majority opinion and perhaps offer some backing for measures taken by individual states. The Uniting for Peace Resolution (General Assembly Resolution 377a (v) 1950), introduced by the United States in the Korean War to circumvent the Soviet veto in the Security Council, allows the General Assembly (if necessary in emergency session) to deal with a problem when the Security Council is stalemated, although the outcome can only be a recommendation. Using the Uniting for Peace procedure, the Assembly branded the People's Republic of China an aggressor in 1951 and recommended additional measures against it and North Korea; the same procedure was followed in January 1980 when the Assembly condemned the Soviet invasion of Afghanistan. Bowett notes that if the Assembly can 'authorize' economic sanctions, 'which was certainly assumed when the Assembly adopted the Uniting for Peace Resolution ...' then 'State action pursuant to an Assembly authorization would ... be justifiable'.[12] But this 'authorization' would not legalise otherwise illegal measures.

One may also argue that unopposed or very heavily supported Assembly resolutions, repeated over a long period of years, establish the acceptance of principles of conduct and develop a cumulative, delegitimising effect on policies of states who flout them. There would be no dispute that South Africa's apartheid system has been definitively characterised as offending against international norms and is now internationally delegitimised. But establishing standards does not produce action and apart from its denial of credentials to the South African delegation since 1974, the Assembly's numerous resolutions calling for sanctions against South Africa are no more than pointers to action for individual UN members who wish to impose such measures to signify their own disapproval in expressive and punitive modes.

It is worth noting that UN specialised agencies are required to support the Security Council in any measures it has ordered.[14] In addition, their governing bodies normally have authority to apply 'internal' penalties if members fail to comply with their rules. In such circumstances, privileges or funds may be withheld, voting rights suspended, and, in serious cases, expulsion is possible. For instance, the General Agreement on Tariffs and Trade (GATT) in Article xxiii (2) permits the contracting parties to suspend concessions under the agreement in certain circumstances. Similarly, the International Monetary Fund's Articles of Agreement allow the governing body to declare a member judged not to be fulfilling its obligations ineligible to use the Fund's general financial resources.[15]

More controversially many UN agencies have followed the spirit of General Assembly recommendations by declaring through a majority vote that South Africa's apartheid policy and its illegal retention of Namibia make it ineligible for continued participation in their work. South Africa has been suspended or forced to withdraw from agencies such as the World Health Organisation (WHO), the International Labour Organisation (ILO) and even the World Meteorological Organisation (WMO), but not from the IMF, World Bank or GATT.[16]

What about the sanctioning authority of regional or other limited membership organisations? The Organisation of American States (OAS) predates the UN, the Arab League was established in 1945, the Organisation of African Unity (OAU) in 1963. These are all regional arrangements which under Chapter viii of the Charter are given limited authority to deal with regional disputes, subject to the overall supervision of the Security Council. The authoritativeness of regional measures is not in question if the Security Council has ordered sanctions. But typically there is no action at the UN level, and this vacuum at the top leaves freedom for the regional body to act.[17] Presumably regional bodies, acting constitutionally, are free to determine rule violation by their members and take appropriate measures. Examples would be the diplomatic and economic sanctions applied by the OAS to Cuba from 1962 to 1975 and the Arab League's suspension of Egypt's membership after the conclusion of the Israeli–Egyptian Peace Treaty in 1979. These cases are discussed in more detail in Chapter 5. Had Greece not withdrawn from the Council of Europe in December 1969, the Council would no doubt have proceeded to suspend it.[18] But there can be serious problems about the legitimacy of sanctions at the regional level, and with the UN in stalemate there is no higher authority to control or even monitor the actions of regional bodies.

In the Western hemisphere the Rio Treaty is the defence 'arm' of the Organisation of American States (OAS) and it contains an explicit commitment on the part of members to respond to an armed attack, thus exercising the right of collective self-defence set out in Article 51 of the UN Charter. But the Rio Treaty also provides in Article 6 that the OAS Organ of Consultation shall meet immediately to agree on measures to be taken for the maintenance of the peace and security of the continent in case of 'aggression which is not an armed attack' or in the face of 'any other fact or situation that might endanger the peace of America'. This Article, which allowed measures to be instituted against the Dominican Republic and Cuba in the 1960s, obviously opens up a grey area in identifying 'aggression' which is not an armed attack, and other (undefined) circumstances which may affect the peace and security of the region.

There is also the problem that regional norms may conflict with universal norms. In 1968, Warsaw Pact military intervention in Czechoslovakia was justified in terms of the Brezhnev Doctrine which purported to assert a norm permitting forceful intervention to preserve socialism.[19] This is certainly not in accordance with general rules of international law regarding the non-use of force and non-intervention. Regional determination of offences, offenders and penalties can obviously reflect the views of a hegemonial power who is able to pressure lesser powers in the region to support it, using carrots and sticks in the process.

In a recent monograph Terry Nardin argues that the international system of states has developed diffused mechanisms for the authoritative determination of rule-breaking.[20] Although this increases uncertainty, just as the absence of centralised enforcement reduces the effectiveness of sanctions, it is unrealistic to ignore what is actually happening. Between the two extremes of unilateral self-help and a mandatory Security Council enforcement order under Chapter VII of the Charter, there is obviously a whole range of possibilities. The picture is made more complex because international bodies may be involved in determining rule violation, in ordering or recommending sanctions, and in actually imposing penalties. And because such intra-organisational determinations are themselves the product of what Nardin calls 'dominant coalitions',[21] objectively they are not necessarily better grounded in generally accepted rules than measures taken outside such frameworks, although formally they may have a more authoritative status. In any case only those sanctions which relate specifically to organisational membership or privileges are self-executing through the organisation in question; others require national implementation.

Outside organisational frameworks, there can also be sanctions, but their justification must be the violation of accepted standards of conduct. The inability of the UN to act in defence of such standards – or even to achieve consensus that they have been violated – diminishes its status and leaves scope for leading powers to assume a responsibility for righting 'wrongs' on a unilateral or multilateral basis.

As Bowett has pointed out, unilateral reprisals differ substantially from 'collective organisational action conceived as a sanction' which involves community action to deal with a threat to or breach of the peace.[22] And it should be noted that the use of a regional or other institutional framework to co-ordinate sanctions against non-members – for instance, European Community sanctions against Argentina – does not *per se* confer authoritativeness on the measures (although it may increase their effectiveness).

In Chapter 1 it was argued that current practice makes too narrow a definition of sanctions counter-productive. Here it can be seen that a broad definition opens up the possibility that authoritativeness or an aura of authoritativeness can be claimed for action which has little or none. Instead of measures which uphold generally accepted standards of behaviour and are linked to acts which violate those standards, the so-called 'sanctions' may be specifically designed to defend or promote the special interests of those imposing them. Regrettably there appears to be no sign of any trend to increased authoritativeness in resort to international sanctions. International 'vigilantism'[23] as the alternative presents some disquieting features which are discussed further in the final chapter of this book. Meanwhile it becomes necessary to examine each case of international sanctions on its merits to see what status can be ascribed to the rule which has been broken – or is alleged to have been broken – and what authority, if any, those imposing sanctions can claim as giving specific backing to their acts. Discretion in almost all cases remains with individual governments regarding both the imposition of sanctions and their implementation and this gives rise to many of the practical problems associated with sanctioning efforts which are discussed further in Chapter 7. First, however, it is necessary to examine the major cases where sanctions have been collectively imposed.

3 League of Nations Sanctions

The procedures outlined in the League Covenant for the imposition of international sanctions were persistently debated, interpreted and reinterpreted during the first 15 years of the League's existence, revealing members' disinclination to be committed in advance to action of this kind. Japan's invasion of Manchuria in 1931 did not lead to League sanctions although a Commission of Enquiry sent by the League Council to study the situation in the Far East reported that Japanese military measures had been unjustified. Recognition of the state of Manchukuo set up by Japan was withheld by the United States and the League but there was no further action. The prolonged Chaco War between Paraguay and Bolivia (1928–38) could also have provided an occasion for a League response but the maximum achieved was a recommendation for an embargo on the sale of arms to both sides.

The announcement of German rearmament in 1935 spurred a League study of ways to improve collective security but Italy, not Germany, became the target of League sanctions following the invasion of Ethiopia by Italian forces in October 1935. In January and again in March of that year, Ethiopia had appealed to the League Council because of a border incident at Walwal involving Italian forces in December 1934 and growing evidence of Italian military preparations in the Horn of Africa.

Britain and France were concerned about Germany's repudiation of its obligations under the Treaty of Versailles and anxious to retain Italian friendship; in the first half of the year they were, therefore, not very responsive to Ethiopia's complaints. But after an arbitration committee had absolved both sides from blame over Walwal, the League Council set Italian–Ethiopian relations as an agenda item for its September meeting. Italy submitted a document describing Ethiopia – a fellow-member of the League – as a barbarous and uncivilised country unable to discharge its obligations under the Covenant, but this could hardly legitimise an Italian 'civilising mission' carried out by force. During September Italy rejected and Ethiopia accepted proposals made by the Council which could have formed the basis for a settlement of their dispute. By this time Italian military preparations were complete. Meanwhile, however, the climate of opinion at Geneva had swung towards decisive action. In Britain the result of the Peace Ballot showed that over ten million respondents supported the use of economic and other non-military measures to check aggression,[1] and the British Foreign Secretary made what was taken to be a firm declaration of loyalty to the League at the Assembly meeting on 11 September, speaking of 'steady and collective resistance to all acts of unprovoked aggression'.

Italy's invasion of Ethiopia on 3 October violated the Covenant which required a delay of three months after publication of a Council report before resorting to war. This violation was promptly confirmed by a Council Committee of Six and led to the automatic application of sanctions under Article 16.

In the second and decisive stage of the crisis Italian forces subdued Ethiopia using all means of modern warfare, including gas, while the members of the League led by Britain, made a show of punishing Italy for its behaviour with some hope perhaps of inducing it to abandon or modify its goal of African expansion.

The sanctions which were imposed by League members comprised an embargo on the export to Italy of arms, munitions, and implements of war; the restriction of financial dealings involving loans, credits, or share issues with Italian government or business concerns; the prohibition of imports from Italy, (with exemptions for books and printed material, gold, silver and coin, goods subject to existing contracts, and goods of Italian origin to which more than 25 per cent of value had been added by processing elsewhere) and a ban on the export to Italy of transport animals, rubber, bauxite, aluminium, iron ore, chromium, manganese, titanium, nickel, tungsten, vanadium and tin. Re-exports to Italy were also banned, but contracts in process of execution and goods already *en route* were exempt. Members also pledged mutual support.[2] 'In nine days' writes Frank Hardie, 'the committee had created, in outline, a new world of international sanctions',[3] and it is true that some fifty members reported that they were applying sanctions by the end of the year, but this was not the complete severance of communication and intercourse laid down in Article 16 of the Covenant, but a much more limited programme of denial which did not include breaking off diplomatic relations or any ban on travel.

Much of the confidence in the League which had been generated by the relatively swift application of sanctions in the autumn of 1935 was lost after the disclosure of the terms of the Hoare–Laval Pact, drawn up privately in Paris in early December by the British Foreign Secretary and the French Prime Minister. The arrangement would have required Ethiopia to cede territory to Italy in the north, and to accept Italian economic expansion and settlement in the south. Although the plan had to be abandoned in the face of public reaction, and Hoare's resignation as Foreign Secretary followed, the damage to the sanctions cause was considerable. The objectives of League action and the support of Britain and France for sanctions were called in question.

League members had acknowledged the expediency of additional export embargoes as soon as the conditions necessary to render this extension effective had been realised. The original list of items was limited to exports controlled by the sanctioning group, due to uncertainty about the policy of the United States and other non-members of the League. Sanctions on oil, and other essential materials such as iron, steel and coal were proposed by the Canadian delegate to the Sanctions Committee in October, but at its January meeting these proposals were abandoned on the grounds that they would be ineffective. However, an expert committee was set up to consider the effectiveness of an oil sanction. In its unanimous report issued on 12 February, this committee made the point that if an embargo on oil were to be universally applied, taking into account Italy's stocks, and supplies *en route*, the impact would be felt only after three and a half months. Moreover, effectiveness could be expected only if all members of the League participated and if the United States restricted its exports to the normal pre-sanctions level.[4]

In the meantime, Italy had made it clear that an oil embargo would be regarded as an act of war and Italian forces were beginning to score military successes in Ethiopia. Once again, events in Europe intervened to divert attention from Africa: Hitler's re-occupation of the Rhineland on 7 March 1936, in breach of the Locarno Treaties and the Treaty of Versailles, led to a meaningless statement from Britain, France and Italy expressing solidarity in the preservation of treaty obligations. Although the General Election held in November 1935 gave the British government electoral support for a firm stand on sanctions, concern not to push Italy into war appears to have been overriding, while France was anxious to retain Italy as an ally against Hitler. Neither Britain nor France was at all enthusiastic about sanctions.

Further efforts organised by the League Council to achieve conciliation between Ethiopia and Italy came to nothing. No extension of sanctions was proposed and the use of gas by Italian forces drew no more than a protest. Events moved swiftly in Ethiopia and on 2 May the Emperor was forced to flee the country. Mussolini declared the war was over and announced the annexation of Ethiopia on 9 May – two days before the next League Council meeting. Consideration of the new state of affairs was postponed for a month while sanctions continued – then the matter was handed to the Assembly to deal with at a special session on 30 June.

The question was whether sanctions should be continued or abandoned and much depended on Britain's attitude. In a speech to Conservative MPs on 10 June, Chancellor of the Exchequer Neville Chamberlain declared any idea that the continuation of sanctions would save Ethiopia to be the 'very midsummer of madness'; the League's function, he said, should be limited and peace be secured by regional arrangements. A week later the Cabinet endorsed this position and it was upheld in the House of Commons by the new Foreign Secretary, Anthony Eden.[5] At Geneva only South Africa and New Zealand were in favour of continuing sanctions; the question of recognising the conquest of Ethiopia was dodged; the reform of the Covenant was canvassed. On 15 July the Sanctions Committee met to recommend the lifting of measures imposed under Article 16.

EFFECTS OF SANCTIONS ON ITALY

Although the economic sanctions applied to Italy were only in place for eight months and their effect was considerably lessened by the political manoeuvres which accompanied them, the League attempt is worth examining briefly as an unprecedented programme of economic restraint imposed in time of peace by a group of fifty nations.

Italy appeared to be especially vulnerable to certain sanctions. Although not markedly deficient in food, and an exporter of manufactures, the country was seriously deficient in raw materials – particularly fuel in the form of coal and mineral oils, cotton and wool for the textile industry, as well as timber, non-ferrous metals, iron and steel, and rubber. An adverse balance of trade was offset in the balance of payments by tourism, emigrants' remittances, and shipping receipts – items which were not eliminated by sanctions. Italy was capable of manufacturing armaments, given the necessary raw materials, and in this respect enjoyed a great advantage over Ethiopia.

In 1934 Italy's leading trade partners were Austria, France, Germany, Switzerland, Britain and the United States. The latter was the dominant supplier of wheat (58 per cent), of cotton and cotton goods (58 per cent), and an important source of iron and steel goods, mineral oils and copper. Germany supplied 47 per cent of Italy's total coal imports, and over 50 per cent of machinery imports. Forty per cent of Italy's steel requirements came from non-members of the League. The only raw material for which League powers were the dominant suppliers was wool, and the economic impact of sanctions was clearly much reduced by the non-cooperation of Austria and Hungary and the neutral policies of the United States, Germany and Switzerland. The United States administration placed an embargo on the export of arms and asked for moral embargoes on trading with the belligerents; Germany embargoed the export of arms to Italy, but otherwise pursued a policy of 'normal' trade.

Figures published by the League show that the ban on exports of strategic raw materials was largely effective by December 1935. But heavy stocks of these commodities, and of oil, had already been built up by Italy, and the fact that military operations in Ethiopia were carried to a successful conclusion showed that the embargoes were not effective. The sanctions might have been more effective if semi-manufactured goods had been included, and if there had been time for them to take effect. As it was, prohibited steel goods came from Germany, Austria and the United States, while permitted goods came from France and the Soviet Union.

Italian exports were well distributed in different markets, but they did not fare well under sanctions. Because of the exemption of contracts in process of execution, the embargoes on Italian goods did not take effect until early in 1936, but a drop in the value of total exports of 50 per cent was recorded in the next few months. These embargoes were intended to aggravate Italy's shortage of foreign exchange, and as a result of the drop in exports, overseas purchasing power was reduced by two-fifths between December 1935 and February 1936, although Italy could still export gold and silver bullion and coin by depleting reserves. Exchange control had been instituted prior to the invasion of Ethiopia. Some re-orientation of foreign trade was achieved, but exports formerly sent to League members were not wholly made up elsewhere. At Italy's expense Germany gained new markets which were retained after sanctions ended.

Official statistics were not published in Italy after September 1935 but the reorganisation of Italian industry by national-isation, and state control of the banking system, instituted in March 1936, indicated strains in the economy. All public issues of capital had to be approved by the Bank of Italy after that date; industry was to work for the armed forces of the state. The lira was devalued by 25 per cent in November 1935. It is likely that Italy lost half her gold reserve between October 1935 and March 1936, but gold was collected internally, and foreign assets could also have been realised.[6]

On 19 May 1936 the Italian Minister of Finance estimated that the import surplus averaged 213 million lira per month between December 1935 and March 1936. 'By the end of the sanctions period it was reckoned that Italy's outstanding commercial debt had mounted to 1500 million lira',[7] and Italy was finding difficulty in paying for goods regardless of source. The Italian balance of payments was showing considerable strain and stocks of raw materials were depleted. One-third of total disposable international assets at the end of September 1935 was realised in the ensuing six months; there was a loss of shipping and tourist receipts, and the heavy cost of the war added to the burden.

As far as financial restraints were concerned, they were not of great significance, as ordinary remittances were not affected, and Italy's lack of credit-worthiness had already made it a poor candidate for loans in the City of London.

Overall, then, the sanctions fulfilled *The Economist*'s prediction that they would be 'highly inconvenient but not crippling'.[8] Renwick makes the interesting point that they brought 'an intensification of government intervention in the economy'[9] and in fact, the lessons to be learned from this ill-fated experiment were largely political. Lack of consensus on the merits of collective action to check aggression was apparent from the earliest days of the League; where sanctions against Italy were concerned, consistent goals were neither clearly stated nor pursued – nor perhaps perceived.

The practical effect of League sanctions was diminished by the failure to embargo vital raw materials or to sever communications. The Suez Canal was left open, tourism was not banned, an air service between Italian Somaliland and Eritrea continued to enjoy landing and refuelling rights in British Somaliland throughout the crisis. It had been secretly agreed by the British and French governments that action against Italy would be limited to non-military measures. Undue reliance may have been placed on the embargo on imports from Italy, which Eden advocated as the key measure which would leave Italy without foreign purchasing power and unable to obtain vital imports, and it is true that uncertainty about the co-operation of the United States and Germany made it difficult to know whether an embargo on strategic materials such as coal, oil, iron and steel would have been effective. It was obvious, however, that if these items were not subject to control, Italy's war-making capacity would not be seriously reduced.[10]

A policy of graduated pressure may have been acceptable on grounds of economy of effort and the avoidance of undue disruption of trade, but it also gave Mussolini the opportunity to declare that extensions to sanctions would be regarded as hostile acts. 'Collective bluffing cannot bring collective security' – the comment of the Canadian Prime Minister at the end of the sanctions experiment[11] – was an apt reflection on the League's experience under British and French leadership. Inaction over Ethiopia might have damaged the League's reputation, but the sanctions venture hardly enhanced it, particularly as the target of collective action not only achieved its goals in triumph, but remained a member of the organisation whose code it had flouted for as long as it chose to do so. In terms of obligations under the Covenant, expulsion of Italy from the League would have been a more appropriate act than discussing whether the Ethiopian delegate had a right to take his seat after the conquest of his country.[12]

The failure of sanctions against Italy accelerated the decline of the League. Attempts to reform it in the years from 1936 to 1939 were concerned more with limiting the obligations which it placed on members than with strengthening its powers, and sterile debates about the respective merits of optional or compulsory sanctions served only to underline the fundamental lack of consensus about the League's true function. Geneva became a political backwater.

The only sanctioning act taken after 1936 came in December 1939, following the Soviet attack on Finland. The League Council voted to expel the USSR, declaring that in terms of Article 16 (4) of the Covenant it had 'placed itself outside the League of Nations'. Eleven members had left the League between 1936 and 1939, and the organisation was inactive during the six years of the Second World War. In April 1946 the League Assembly met for the last time and by unanimous vote the League of Nations was formally dissolved. Its successor organisation, the United Nations, was already in existence.

4   United Nations Sanctions

Despite the elaborate enforcement provisions of Chapter VII of the Charter, and forty years of life, the UN record of sanctioning is sparse. As far as mandatory sanctions are concerned, the only important case is Rhodesia (now Zimbabwe); a minor instance is the embargo on arms sales to South Africa which has been in force since 1977. Other measures have been adopted voluntarily, pursuant to recommendations made by UN organs. In the Korean case the Security Council made the initial recommendations for military measures and there have also been Security Council recommendations for a ban on the sale of arms to Portugal for use in its overseas territories, on arms sales to Rhodesia prior to the imposition of mandatory sanctions and for voluntary economic sanctions against South Africa. In other instances the General Assembly has been the source of encouragement for sanctions imposition. In 1946 it recommended that members should sever diplomatic relations with the Franco regime because of its pro-Axis stand during the Second World War, and subsequently there were recommendations in respect of North Korea and the People's Republic of China, but the main focus of attention has been Southern Africa: Portugal till 1974; Rhodesia until 1980, and South Africa as a continuing issue. There have also been moves in the General Assembly to organise penalties against Israel but these have been vigorously opposed by the United States which took strong exception to the 1975 Assembly resolution declaring Zionism to be 'a form of racism and racial discrimination' and threatened retaliation if action were taken against Israel in the UN or its agencies.[1] In some recent cases, Security Council and/or General Assembly condemnation without reference to sanctions has been forthcoming, but these cases belong in a later chapter. Here we are concerned only with penalties which have been ordered or recommended by the UN.

A brief account of the Korean case is in order as it represented the first test of collective measures under the provisions of Chapter VII. The North Korean attack on South Korea in June 1950 led to a Security Council decision that a breach of peace had occurred. An immediate cessation of hostilities was called for and members were specifically asked to assist the Republic of South Korea in repelling armed attack and thus restoring international peace and security in the area (Resolutions 82, 25 June; 83, 27 June 1950). No veto was forthcoming from the Soviet Union which was boycotting Council meetings because of the failure to seat representatives of the People's Republic of China. The Council had no power to make participation in the military effort compulsory because agreements covering the use of force have never been concluded under Article 43 of the Charter. Military measures were organised under United States command and with the United States providing the bulk of the force. Willingness to support collective security in principle was expressed by 53 nations but only 16 offered military contingents.

The intervention of Communist China on the side of North Korea in October of the same year posed new problems, particularly as the Soviet Union had resumed attendance at Security Council meetings and vetoed further action. The matter was transferred to the General Assembly which, acting under the Uniting for Peace Resolution, tried without success to effect conciliation and then passed a resolution naming China an aggressor. A Good Offices Committee was charged with the duty of seeking a peaceful solution, while an Additional Measures Committee was to report on further measures that could be taken. By May 1951 it was clear that peaceful settlement was not possible, and the Assembly recommended 'additional' economic measures comprising an embargo on shipment to areas controlled by Communist China and North Korea of arms, ammunition and implements of war, atomic energy materials, petroleum, transportation materials of strategic value, and items useful for producing military materiel (Resolution 500 (v), 18 May 1951). This general embargo was already broadly effective in so far as Western powers were concerned under existing strategic embargoes on trade with Communist countries; naturally, the Soviet bloc did not support the resolution. The first United Nations experiment with collective measures of an economic nature was therefore incomplete, indecisive and inconclusive. The embargoes were not formally authorised by the UN, were ancillary to the military effort and could be of only limited effect since China could, at that time, obtain military equipment from the Soviet Union and other Communist countries. The Korean armistice in July 1953 brought an end to all United Nations measures, though not to the Western embargoes.

Over the next two decades there were numerous crises particularly in the Middle East, the Congo and Cyprus, in which UN peacekeeping efforts were organised with the consent of the parties involved. Enforcement under Chapter VII of the Charter was discussed within the UN almost exclusively in relation to Southern Africa where Portuguese colonialism, the entrenchment of white minority rule in Rhodesia, and South Africa's apartheid system and continuing administration of Namibia came under increasing criticism from the growing Third World membership. The following section reviews the record of the UN in Southern Africa to the end of 1985.

(a) Portugal

Beginning in 1961 the General Assembly passed a series of resolutions calling for economic sanctions against Portugal with the object of inducing the Portuguese government to accept the principle of self-determination for the inhabitants of its African territories. In 1965 the Assembly recommended that a wide range of sanctions should be imposed, including the breaking of diplomatic relations, the closing of ports to Portuguese vessels, and a boycott of trade; in 1966 that the Security Council should apply sanctions against Portugal under Chapter VII of the Charter. Western powers did not support this view, and the Security Council merely passed two recommendatory resolutions calling for a ban on the sale or shipment of arms and military equipment, and of materials for manufacture of military materiel which could be used for the suppression of indigenous people in Portuguese Overseas African Territories (Resolutions 180, 31 July 1963; 218, 23 November 1965). There is no evidence that these recommendations were carried out by United Nations members, or that Portuguese policy was modified as a result of them. For Western countries, strategic and trade links with a fellow-member of NATO took precedence over concern about Portugal's colonial policy.

The catalyst for change in the Portuguese African territories was the mounting strain of full-scale guerrilla warfare in both Angola and Mozambique and increasing discontent in Portugal itself, culminating in the coup which ousted the Salazar regime in April 1974. Independence for Angola and Mozambique in 1975, though not free from continuing violence in the former case, brought an end to white rule and thus to censure at the UN.

(b) Rhodesia (now Zimbabwe)

The Rhodesian case is unique in the record of the United Nations in that a wide range of mandatory economic sanctions was imposed by the Security Council under Chapter VII of the Charter to deal with a situation defined as constituting a threat to the peace.

The unilateral declaration of independence by the Rhodesian government on 11 November 1965 followed months of negotiation with Britain on the question of the territory's constitutional future, while at meetings of the United Nations, the Commonwealth and the Organisation of African Unity there was continued pressure on Britain not only to forestall or prevent UDI, but to assume a more direct responsibiity for African political advancement in Rhodesia.

It is not necessary in this context to relate the history of the short-lived Federation of Rhodesia and Nyasaland which was finally dissolved at the end of 1963.[2] It is relevant, however, to summarise briefly the issues at stake, which led to the voluntary imposition of sanctions by Britain and many other countries immediately after UDI and, one year later, to mandatory UN sanctions.

The break-up of the Federation was followed in 1964 by the independence and admission to the Commonwealth and UN of Zambia (formerly Northern Rhodesia) and Malawi (formerly Nyasaland), both ruled by African governments. (Southern) Rhodesia which had enjoyed full internal self-government since 1923 with white minority rule, came out of Federation well in material terms, but independence was to be granted only when African participation in government was further advanced. In the meantime the 1961 Constitution, which gave limited and qualified franchise to Africans, was to continue in force. The black population in 1965 was approximately 4 million; the whites numbered some 250 000. Independence was the declared aim of the Rhodesian Front Party, led by Ian Smith, which eliminated the Parliamentary Opposition in the elections of May 1965. A referendum in November 1964 had produced an 89 per cent vote in favour of independence, although only 60 per cent of the electorate voted; this followed a warning from the newly elected Labour government in Britain that an illegal declaration of independence by Southern Rhodesia would cut it off from Britain, the Commonwealth, most foreign governments and international organisations, and bring immediate economic retaliation.

Negotiations with the British government on the independence issue centred around five principles which Britain insisted must be accepted. A sixth principle was added by Prime Minister Harold Wilson in January 1966, after UDI. These principles required unimpeded progress to majority rule; guarantees against retrogressive amendment of the Constitution; immediate improvement in the political status of the African population and progress towards ending racial discrimination; acceptance by the people of Rhodesia as a whole of any formula for independence; no oppression of majority by minority or of minority by majority.[3]

Stalemate was reached in the autumn of 1965, in spite of a personal visit to Salisbury by Mr Wilson, and the atmosphere of crisis mounted in early November when the Rhodesian government declared a three-month State of Emergency and imposed general import controls. On 11 November, UDI was announced, thus confronting the British government with a *fait accompli*.

Official reaction in Britain was sharp. On the same day Mr Wilson condemned the act as illegal and ineffective in law, terming it an act of rebellion against Crown and Constitution and instructing the Governor of Rhodesia to inform the Rhodesian Prime Minister and his colleagues that they no longer held office. On paper, the British government took over full responsibility for the government of Rhodesia; legislative and executive authority was vested in the Crown (i.e. the Imperial government) in terms of the Southern Rhodesia Act passed on 16 November. But no use of force was contemplated. The Prime Minister had already stated categorically in the British House of Commons that under no circumstances would Britain assert military power, whether to suspend or amend the 1961 Constitution, to impose majority rule 'tomorrow or any other time' or to deal 'with the situation that would follow an illegal assertion of independence'.[4]

Britain took the lead in imposing economic measures which were announced progressively in the three months following UDI. A complete ban on imports into British territories of Rhodesian tobacco was imposed on 11 November, together with a ban on further purchases of Rhodesian sugar. Exports of petroleum and petroleum products were banned on 17 December 1965, a total ban on exports to Rhodesia, (excepting only items of a humanitarian nature, books, films, requirements for Central African organisations, and goods on quays already paid for), was in force by 30 January 1966, and a total ban on imports by the end of February. Penalties wre prescribed for illegal trading.

Financial measures included the removal of Rhodesia from the sterling area; its exclusion from membership of the Commonwealth preference area and the Commonwealth Sugar Agreement; the end of British financial aid; the prohibition of the export of capital to Rhodesia; and the closing of the London capital market for Rhodesian dealings. Current payments by residents of the United Kingdom to Rhodesia were virtually stopped; Rhodesian sterling was blocked and could no longer be exchanged for foreign currency in Britain. Assets of the Rhodesian Reserve Bank, amounting to approximately £10 million were frozen in London; the governor and directors were suspended and a new board appointed in Britain.

Commonwealth and other countries followed Britain's lead in severing or reducing economic links with Rhodesia. The Council of Ministers of the Organisation of African Unity announced a total economic boycott in December 1965, which included a ban on communication and denial of overflying rights. The United States and France imposed oil embargoes in December 1965 and the former also banned exports to Rhodesia in March 1966; France imposed restrictions on the import of tobacco and sugar.

In spite of these harsh economic measures, and the denial of recognition to the government of Rhodesia, it remained in full administrative control. Its practical competence was acknowledged by all Rhodesians from the outset and, subsequently, by the British government itself which on numerous occasions conducted negotiations for a settlement with the Smith regime.

There was strong external pressure on Britain to take the matter to the United Nations. At a special Commonwealth Conference in Lagos in January 1966, Harold Wilson confidently (and inaccurately) predicted that measures taken by his government would restore legality in Rhodesia 'within a matter of weeks rather than months'.[5] At a second Commonwealth Conference in London in the following September, Britain was pressed by African members to take more drastic action, and agreed that if the Rhodesian government did not take steps to end the rebellion by the end of the year, Britain would withdraw previous offers for a constitutional settlement, would not consider granting independence before majority rule and would take the matter to the Security Council. As further efforts to find a negotiated solution proved fruitless, the British government reluctantly followed this course of action in December 1966 and the Security Council voted to impose economic sanctions on 16 December (Resolution 232). Although the measures selected were not as extensive as those already in force on a voluntary basis in Britain and other Commonwealth and non-Commonwealth countries, they were mandatory for all United Nations members. Sanctions against Rhodesia would therefore provide the first real test of United Nations 'enforcement' using economic weapons.

Rhodesia had featured on United Nations agenda since 1962. Immediately prior to UDI, the Assembly had called upon Britain to employ all necessary measures, including military force, to deal with rebellion by the Smith government; after UDI the Security Council called upon all states to cease providing the illegal regime with arms, equipment and military materiel, 'and to do their utmost in order to break all economic relations with Southern Rhodesia'. An embargo on the export of petroleum and petroleum products was particularly recommended (Resolution 217, 20 November 1965).

In April 1966, at the request of the British government, and in order to prevent oil reaching Rhodesia via the port of Beira, the Security Council invoked Article 39 of the Charter, authorising Britain to intercept ships bound for Beira which were reasonably believed to be carrying oil destined for Rhodesia and prevent them from discharging their cargo, by force if necessary (Resolution 221, 9 April 1966).

The grounds for collective action against the rebel regime in

Rhodesia were provided by Britain's decision, supported by resolutions of the Security Council and the General Assembly, that the rebellion was not only an illegal act, which should be put down by the constitutional authority (Britain), but one which had international implications and was legitimately the concern of the United Nations as a threat to the peace. That Britain acknowledged this fact was clear from warnings that it would take the matter to the United Nations if the Rhodesian government did not come to terms; its subsequent recourse to the Security Council for authority to establish a blockade of Beira confirmed it. The decision to impose mandatory sanctions under Articles 39 and 41 was taken with Britain's concurring vote, while France and the Soviet Union abstained. Politically, no permanent member had an interest in using the veto.

The sanctions imposed by Resolution 232 banned the export of petroleum, arms, ammunition and military equipment, vehicles and aircraft to Rhodesia and imports from Rhodesia of tobacco, sugar, meat and meat products, asbestos, copper, chrome ore, iron ore, hides and skins – key commodities which made up 59 per cent by value of her export trade. Non-recognition of Rhodesia's self-styled independence continued to be universal.

In the face of continued defiance by the Smith regime, sanctions were intensified in May 1968 to comprise a total ban on imports of Rhodesian origin and on exports to Rhodesia (except for medical and educational material and equipment); a complete ban on the transfer of funds to Rhodesia for investment for government or private purposes; non-acceptability of Rhodesian passports for travel; the severance of air links and the withdrawal of consular and trade representation in Rhodesia. In addition a Committee of the Security Council was established to monitor the implementation of sanctions (Resolution 253, 29 May 1968).

Resolution 253 appeared to close the loopholes left by Resolution 232, but South Africa and Portugal continued to trade openly and to maintain air communciations with Rhodesia. A further crisis at the UN was provoked in 1970 when the Smith regime introduced a republican constitution which worsened the position of Rhodesian blacks. In the Security Council Britain and the United States used their veto power (the latter for the first time) to block the extension of sanctions to Portugal and

South Africa. Meanwhile, the Conservative government led by Edward Heath, which was in power in Britain from 1970 to 1974, sponsored another round of negotiations with the Rhodesian regime. This produced proposals which the Pearce Commission put to the African people of Rhodesia in 1972, and which they in turn rejected. The Commission reported that the Africans were prepared to pay the price of suffering the main burden of sanctions in order to achieve majority rule.[6] Rhodesia continued to resist international censure and defy sanctions with some success. But the sands were running out for Portuguese rule in Angola and Mozambique and the coup in Portugal in 1974 was to usher in an era in which not only Rhodesia, but also South Africa, would be exposed to new and powerful pressures. Guerrilla warfare began in Rhodesia in 1972, placing new strains on the economy and on white morale, while the withdrawal of South African police forces from Rhodesia in 1975 signalled an obvious preference in Pretoria for a settlement in Rhodesia which would satisfy Britain and the US – even if that meant majority rule.[7] By 1976 Ian Smith was ready to accept a transitional multi-racial government and majority rule within two years in return for the lifting of sanctions and the end of guerrilla warfare, but guerrilla warfare could not be turned off like a tap. The forces of Joshua Nkomo and Robert Mugabe, loosely associated in the Patriotic Front, had goals of their own which could only be met by military means and the war continued to escalate. Its cost in terms of human life was 12 000 dead by the end of 1978, nearly one half in that year alone; agricultural regions were under attack and a number of serious incidents of terrorism, including the shooting down of Air Rhodesia planes and a fire in the Salisbury oil depot estimated to have cost about £10 million in foreign exchange had brought the war to the heart of 'white' Rhodesia. Smith's so-called 'internal settlement' in Rhodesia led to the election of a black majority in Parliament and a government head by a black Prime Minister (Bishop Muzorewa) in March 1978. The official name was changed to Zimbabwe–Rhodesia. But guerrilla war continued unabated and Rhodesia's neighbours, particularly Zambia, were suffering badly as a rseult of spillover effects of sanctions. At the Lusaka Conference of Commonwealth Heads of Government in August 1979 pressure from other Commonwealth leaders persuaded Prime Minister Margaret Thatcher, whose Conservative government had taken office in May, that acceptance of the internal settlement by Britain and the unilateral lifting of sanctions (which was being advocated in right-wing Tory circles) would be asking for more trouble.[8] The Lancaster House Conference, called in late September, brought together as full participants the British government, the government of Bishop Muzorewa and the leaders of the Patriotic Front. In December, after very difficult negotiations, agreement was reached on a constitutional settlement, a cease fire, and transitional arrangements for the pre-independence period.[9]

Rhodesia then reverted to the status of a British colony under the rule of a Governor until elections under universal suffrage could be held. The new constitution reserved 20 seats for whites in the 100 member House of Assembly, with safeguards against constitutional change for a seven-year period. A small force of 2000 British and Commonwealth personnel supervised the cease fire; the elections in February 1980, monitored by a Commonwealth Observer Group, produced a clear victory for the ZANU party, led by Robert Mugabe, who became Prime Minister of an independent Zimbabwe on 18 April. In Resolution 460 of 21 December 1979, the Security Council had already lifted sanctions, a move anticipated by Britain on 12 December and the United States on 16 December.

EFFECTS OF SANCTIONS ON RHODESIA (ZIMBABWE)

As in the Italian case, it is worth commenting briefly on the sanctions programme. For as long as sanctions were the main source of pressure on the white minority regime they obviously did not end UDI; what can be said about their contribution to the final outcome?

At UDI, the Rhodesian economy had certain built-in strengths: a subsistence agriculture sector (which supported about half the African population) and attainable self-sufficiency in food; considerable mineral resources including chrome ore and gold; an industrial base which could be rapidly expanded to utilise unused capacity; hydro-electric power in abundance. Its weaknesses were its landlocked position and dependence on foreign transport routes; dependence on foreign trade for 38 per cent of national income; concentration of export earnings on a few commodities, notably tobacco, and two markets (Britain and South Africa); the need to import petroleum which in 1965 represented 28 per cent of total energy requirements; and the numerical insignificance of the white population who wielded economic and political power but were outnumbered at least eight to one by Africans (a ratio which was worsening). While all sections of the population suffered some hardship under sanctions, the government was particularly concerned to protect whites who were the source of electoral support: compensation schemes and other forms of financial assistance helped to maintain farmers' incomes. The African population took the brunt of sanctions and the steadily growing level of African unemployment became a serious strain on the economy. The increasing rate of white emigration, in spite of stringent controls on removal of assets, also weakened the economy as time passed.

Rhodesia's export trade was concentrated in the relatively small range of primary commodities which were listed in Security Council Resolution No. 232 of 1966, but the sanctions were never fully effective and as time passed they became less so. Tobacco pre-UDI accounted for 30 per cent by value of Rhodesia's export trade ($132 million out of a total of $399 million in 1965) and as half the crop traditionally went to British markets, it was seen as a prime target for sanctions. Initially it was very badly hit and the Rhodesian government took urgent measures to assist farmers to stockpile while encouraging diversification into other crops. Sugar, like tobacco was placed under sanction by Britain in 1965, and here too, exports suffered at first, but agricultural exports, especially beef and beef products, continued to find markets and the diversification of production, particularly into maize and wheat, also strengthened Rhodesia's export trade. Minerals, particularly asbestos, nickel and chrome were exported via South Africa; from 1971 to 1977 the United States openly violated UN sanctions by importing chrome ore from Rhodesia under the Byrd amendment, the alternative being to import it from the USSR. Overall, the UN Secretariat concluded that in spite of sanctions Rhodesia was able 'to send its exports indirectly to world markets'.[10]

Rhodesia's import trade was more widely diversified than her export trade; the commodities listed in the original sanctions resolutions – (motor vehicles and parts, petroleum and petroleum products, and aircraft and parts) – were 'strategic' items, but they accounted for only 16 per cent of total Rhodesian imports in 1965. It was obviously in the interests of the regime to keep the import bill as low as possible, and to use foreign currency for essential purposes. Sanctions gave a strong impetus to import substitution and the further development of manufacturing industry. Pre-UDI industrial activity was concentrated mainly in processing and packing of agricultural products, in textiles and clothing and the manufacture of building materials; there was also some output of furniture, paints and electrical appliances. After UDI manufacturers concentrated on the home market, and in addition to expanding the lines noted above, new consumer products were developed. Locally grown cotton provided a base for the rapid growth of the textile and clothing industry. But the small home market and the limits set on exports by sanctions made it impossible for Rhodesian industry to continue to expand. Moreover, Rhodesia needed to import some capital goods and here sanctions presented difficulties and added to costs.

From the beginning, foreign exchange was a serious problem for the Smith regime and stringent controls were imposed. Rhodesian currency was convertible only in South Africa and this forced a variety of schemes for obtaining much needed foreign currency or doing without it.[11] Exporting at a discount and importing at a premium added to the problem. In the early years after UDI, the blocking of financial transactions by Britain and later by the United Nations worked to Rhodesia's advantage in that it was able to repudiate external debts and retain dividends and profits within the country, but the need for foreign capital for development outstripped profits (which had to be reinvested locally because of sanctions) plus what was available from South African sources. In 1965 tourism was the largest foreign exchange earner after tobacco, asbestos and copper and for some years the tourist industry held up well in spite of sanctions. But the insecurity produced by guerrilla warfare and terrorism dealt a blow to Rhodesia's tourist trade in the late 1970s.

The effects of sanctions were offset by defensive and adaptive measures taken by the Rhodesian government and supported by the white population, and by the capacity of the economy to respond to new needs. But it must also be recognised that sanctions evasion was an important factor with Portugal (until

1974) and South Africa playing a crucial role. The vital commodity was probably petroleum, and here the UN oil embargo was circumvented from the outset. Supplies were made available from South Africa on an emergency basis, and neither the closing of the Beira–Umtali pipeline (and the Ferukka refinery in Rhodesia) nor the limited blockade of Beira from April 1966 which was followed by the Security Council's decision to include petroleum among banned exports in December 1966, succeeded in depriving the Rhodesian economy of adequate supplies of refined petroleum. Reports commissioned by the Commonwealth Committee on Southern Africa in 1977[12] and the British government in 1978 (the Bingham Report)[13] revealed the existence of 'swap' (product exchange) arrangements between the oil companies and their subsidiaries in Mozambique and South Africa. Initially supplies went by road over Beit Bridge; between February 1966 and March 1967 oil products were carried by rail from South Africa to Rhodesia via Mozambique; from 1967 to 1975 supplies went by rail, in bond, from Lourenço Marques to Rhodesia. After that the new Rhodesia–South Africa direct rail link was used. The Bingham Report noted that the British government was aware of the scale of supply to Rhodesia as early as May 1966 and attempted to check it, but the non-cooperation of South Africa and Portugal made this impossible, unless an embargo on oil supplies to South Africa and Mozambique were also imposed. The British government concentrated its attention on 'achieving a position in which it could truly be said that British companies were not engaged in supplying Rhodesia and that no British oil was reaching Rhodesia'.[14] But the Beira blockade was not extended to Lourenço Marques (now called Maputo).

Foreign trade was also maintained in other commodities, although with difficulty and at increased cost. From the time it was set up in 1968, the Security Council Sanctions Committee complained of the difficulty of determining the true origin of goods suspected as being 'Rhodesian' but carrying documentation certifying export from other sources. It proved equally difficult to determine whether Rhodesia was the ultimate destination of goods legally exported to the South African Customs Union (or to Portugal and Mozambique before the mid-1970s).

Most of the cases of alleged sanctions evasion handled by the Security Council Sanctions Committee prior to 1973 were reported by Britain, and the majority of prosecutions for sanctions breaking were in Britain and the United States. After 1973, information from non-governmental bodies, particularly the London *Sunday Times* and various church groups, enabled the Committee to expose an air link between Rhodesia and Europe which used Gabon as a staging post, and various other illegal operations, but clearly the Committee's information was limited and governments were reluctant to follow up Committee allegations.

In seeking to make an overall assessment of the effects of sanctions on the Rhodesian situation, it is hard to disentangle cause and effect.[15] From 1965 first British and then UN sanctions obviously had a direct and generally adverse effect on the economy, particularly by hitting Rhodesia's export trade which brought a serious shortage of foreign exchange. But there was much adaptability and resilience and to the extent that economic sanctions stimulated agriculture and diversification they might possibly have been viewed as useful and certainly not fulfilling the hopes of their backers. Similarly, Rhodesia's greatly enhanced dependence on South Africa which brought close economic integration was not a preferred outcome, and the disposition to negotiate an acceptable settlement may have been lessened by the mood of defiance and by the development of vested interests in the continuation of sanctions which marked the white Rhodesian scene.

But from the mid-1970s the situation in Rhodesia clearly deteriorated steadily. It was not that sanctions *per se* were more effective, although some of the predicted long-term effects of inability to maintain employment opportunities for increasing numbers of black school-leavers were beginning to be felt in both economic and political terms. Rather, external developments posed new and serious problems.

The first oil shock was followed by an international recession, while changes in the political configuration of the Southern African region were much to the disadvantage of the Smith regime. And all commentators agree that the steadily escalating level of guerrilla warfare inside Rhodesia had a devastating effect on the economy and on white morale. Statistics covering economic performance during the sanctions years are now available from the Zimbabwe Statistical Office. Perhaps the most telling are figures of white migration which still showed a small net gain in 1975 but showed a net loss of 41 246 for the years 1976–9. For a total white population of some 260 000 this was very serious indeed.[16]

Taking the full range of economic restrictions in conjunction with the isolation of Rhodesia from the international community, and the universal non-recognition of its independent status, one must ascribe a cumulatively damaging effect to the overall UN programme. In the early years, the Smith regime hoped for a 'withering away' of isolation; not only would economic sanctions break down (and here the Byrd amendment gave undue grounds for optimism) but international political acceptance would gradually come about. This proved a serious miscalculation of the calibre and tenacity of the forces ranged against Rhodesia, which were to grow stronger, not weaker, in terms both of moral credibility and of the economic strength of many of the third world countries whose goodwill Britain and other western powers could not afford to forfeit. Over fifteen years, the UN norms of non-discrimination and majority rule progressively delegitimised the Rhodesian and South African concepts of white minority rule and apartheid. Sanctions against Rhodesia, while not bringing an immediate result, contributed to the process of undermining white rule there (and in Southern Africa as a whole) but the guerrilla war, the independence of Angola and Mozambique, and pressure from South Africa for a settlement were probably of greater direct significance.

(c) The Republic of South Africa

To complete the record of UN sponsored sanctions requires mention of South Africa which is now in an unenviable position as the only example of constitutionally-entrenched white minority rule in the world. As noted in Chapter 1, persistent internal unrest in South Africa in 1985 brought the country and its problems back into the spotlight of world attention. The anti-apartheid movement in the west gained new supporters and new strength, and western governments for the first time not only accepted in principle the appropriateness of sanctions as a means of bringing pressure to bear on the South African government, but also took some small practical steps of an economic and political nature. This chapter gives a brief account of UN action taken by the General Assembly and specialised agencies and the Security Council to the end of 1985; more detailed consideration of the problems which South Africa poses for the international community in general and for western governments in particular is reserved for a later chapter.

Both apartheid and the status of Namibia (the former mandate South-West Africa) have featured prominently in discussion at the United Nations from its earliest days. The South African system blatantly denies human rights to inhabitants who do not have white skins and it would be technically possible, given consensus in the Security Council, to designate the internal situation in South Africa, or indeed the issue of Namibia, a threat to the peace and to order sanctions under Chapter VII of the Charter. That this has not happened is not for want of Third World campaigning. As the UN and the Commonwealth came to include an increasing number of new Asian and African states, pressure mounted to exclude South Africa from international institutions and to punish it for its inhumane policies. Faced with this hostile attitude, South Africa withdrew from the Commonwealth on becoming a republic in 1961 and resigned or was excluded from a number of regional and functional agencies, including the UN Economic Commission for Africa, UNESCO, FAO and the ILO.

The General Assembly has passed countless resolutions condemning South Africa's apartheid policy and after the disturbances in Sharpeville and other South African towns in 1960, the Security Council also took up the issue. Resolution 134 of 1 April 1960 laid the blame for African loss of life on the South African government's racial policies; recognising that the situation might endanger international peace and security it called upon the South African government to abandon apartheid. Britain and France abstained from voting. Measures amounting to sanctions were first recommended by the General Assembly in 1962 when members were requested to break diplomatic relations with South Africa (or refrain from establishing them), to sever shipping and air links and to boycott South African trade. By the same resolution, the Assembly established the Special Committee on Apartheid to keep the racial policies of the South African government under continuous review and requested the Security Council to take appropriate measures, including sanctions and not excluding expulsion, to secure South Africa's compliance with UN resolutions (Resolution 1761 (xvii), 6 November 1962).

In 1963, the Security Council followed up the Assembly's action with a resolution which described the situation in South Africa as 'seriously disturbing' international peace and security (avoiding the precise terminology of Article 39) and solemnly called on all states to cease forthwith the sale and shipment to South Africa of arms, ammunition of all types, and military vehicles (Resolution 181, 7 August 1963). A proposal for a trade boycott was defeated. In December the Security Council reiterated its call for a ban on arms sales to South Africa, adding equipment and materials for the manufacture of arms to the list. It also authorised the Secretary-General to appoint a group of experts to examine methods of resolving the South African problem (Resolution 182, 4 December 1963). Britain and France qualified their position on the arms embargo, stating that they would distinguish between items to be used for internal suppression and items to be used for external defence; the latter would continue to be supplied. The Labour government which took office in Britain in October 1964, banned all arms exports to South Africa immediately.

In April 1964, the report of the Group of Experts recommended a National Convention 'fully representative of the whole population of South Africa' to set a new course for the future – a proposal which was promptly rejected by the South African government. The Group also recommended an expert examination of the economic and strategic aspects of sanctions. Acting on this suggestion, the Security Council reaffirmed its call for all members to observe the ban on the sale of military equipment, and set up an Expert Committee to study the feasibility of sanctions against South Africa. It was clear from the deliberations of this Committee that South Africa's major trading partners were opposed to any programme of economic restraints, and this continued to be their position until well into the 1980s.

The Organisation of African Unity, established in 1963, had also recommended sanctions against South Africa to its members; diplomatic links were severed – or not established, trade was officially boycotted, and overflying rights denied to South African planes.

The South African government's refusal to place the mandated territory of South-West Africa (renamed Namibia by the

UN in 1968) under international trusteeship or to grant it independence, and its failure to apply mandatory sanctions to Rhodesia provided further grounds for international censure. In 1966, following the World Court's decision that Ethiopia and Liberia had not demonstrated sufficient material legal interest to bring their case challenging South Africa's administration of Namibia before the Court,[17] the General Assembly voted 114:2 with 3 abstentions, to terminate the mandate for Namibia and place the territory under UN administration (Resolution 2145 (xxi) 21 October 1966). The Assembly's action was upheld in subsequent Security Council resolutions (276, 30 January 1970; 284, 29 July 1970) and by an Advisory Opinion given by the Court at the Security Council's request in June 1971, which confirmed the illegality of South Africa's continued presence in the territory.[18]

However, South Africa went ahead with its own plans to give Namibia independence under a constitution which guaranteed continued white dominance. This was not acceptable to the South West African People's Organisation (SWAPO) which is recognised by the UN as representing the African people of Namibia, or to the international community, and guerrilla warfare has continued in the territory. South African forces pulled out of Angola in 1985, but objections to the presence of Cuban forces there are still cited as one obstacle to a settlement in Namibia.

South Africa's support for Rhodesia and failure to apply UN sanctions was noted earlier in this Chapter and this aroused further resentment and condemnation at the UN. In November 1974 a vote of 91:22 in the General Assembly confirmed its President's rejection of the credentials of the South Africa delegation but a triple veto of Britain, France and the United States blocked a Security Council resolution for South Africa's expulsion. However, in 1976 riots and repression in black townships led to Security Council Resolution 418 of 4 November 1977 which declared the arms trade with South Africa 'a threat to the peace' under Article 39 of the Charter and ordered a mandatory arms embargo to be universally applied. The resolution is self-liquidating; presumably compliance by members, who are legally bound by the terms of the resolution, would end the threat. Apartheid itself has been called by many names and denounced on innumerable occasions and the UN General

Assembly proclaimed 1982 the 'International Year of Mobilisation for Sanctions' against South Africa, but western powers were still not prepared to support an Article 39 determination that it was a threat to the peace which required mandatory sanctions. On taking office in 1980, the Reagan Administration launched a policy of 'constructive engagement' with the object of bringing friendly pressure to bear on the South African government, and negotiations on Namibia have continued intermittently and so far unsuccessfully through the so-called Contact Group (the United States, Canada, Britain, France and West Germany) to devise a formula for free and fair elections in Namibia with SWAPO participating, as called for in Security Council Resolution 385 of 30 January 1976.

In 1984 the South African government introduced constitutional changes which allow direct elections to three legislative chambers by Whites, Coloureds, and Asians, and in 1985 certain particularly offensive pieces of legislation (notably the Mixed Marriages and Immorality Acts) were repealed, but blacks still have no vote except in the so-called 'homelands' whose patently suprious independence has failed to win any outside recognition. The inauguration of the new constitution provoked renewed protest in South Africa and internal unrest, which continues at the time of writing, led to the proclamation of a State of Emergency in numerous areas of the country in July 1985. A mounting toll of death and destruction brought renewed calls for radical reform of the system – and for sanctions – from unofficial and official external sources. France took the initiative in the Security Council in late July, introducing a resolution which condemned the State of Emergency, called for the end of apartheid and recommended voluntary, selective sanctions by UN members. Resolution 569 was adopted on 26 July by a vote of 13 to none, with Britain and the United States abstaining. An amendment proposed by Burkina Faso which threatened measures under Chapter VII was vetoed by these two powers, with France abstaining.

Subsequent developments in the second half of 1985 included action on a number of fronts. In the United States, Congress proposed legislation to sever certain commercial and financial links with South Africa, and this led President Reagan to modify his previous stance of total opposition to sanctions and impose some mild measures. These comprised a ban on computer exports to South Africa security forces and agencies involved in the enforcement of apartheid; a ban on loans except for those contributing to housing and health projects open to all races; a ban on the export of nuclear goods and technology except what is required under International Atomic Energy Agency (IAEA) rules or for health and safety. The President's Executive order signed in September also prohibited the import of military materiel from South Africa, banned government export assistance to US companies employing more than 25 people in South Africa who did not sign the Sullivan code of conduct, and promised consultation with parties to the General Agreement on Tariffs and Trade (GATT) with a view to banning the import of Krugerrands to the United States.[19] In an obvious effort to minimise the extent of the policy change, Secretary of State Schultz said in a Press briefing that these were not sanctions but 'actions designed to register our view against apartheid, as distinct from actions designed to have an effect by depriving people in South Africa of economic livelihood'.[20]

In the same month the Foreign Ministers of the European Community plus Spain and Portugal agreed on 'restrictive measures' which preclude military co-operation and new collaboration in nuclear sectors; ban the export of oil; ban exports of sensitive equipment for use by the South African police; discourage cultural and scientific agreements except where these contribute towards the ending of apartheid, and freeze official contacts and international agreements in the sporting and security spheres.[21] These measures were to be accompanied by positive steps to give assistance to non-violent anti-apartheid organisations and to reinforce the Community Code of Conduct for firms operating in South Africa.[22] It was agreed that the situation would be re-examined within a reasonable period if there was no significant progress in dismantling apartheid.

Britain reluctantly went along with its EC partners in these actions despite the Prime Minister's publicly stated opposition to sanctions.[23] At the Commonwealth Heads of Government meeting in Nassau, Bahamas, in October, Mrs Thatcher came under concerted pressure to take some action against the South African government which would both express repugnance and also contribute to the economic difficulties which South Africa was already experiencing due to a general erosion of confidence in the stability and future prospects of the economy. This loss of confidence had already produced a dramatic fall in the value of the rand in terms of other currencies and in September the South African authorities introduced a moratorium on foreign debt repayment until December 1985 (which was further extended into 1986).

The outcome of the Commonwealth meeting was a decision to take 'a number of measures which have as their rationale impressing on the authorities in Pretoria the compelling urgency of dismantling apartheid and erecting the structures of democracy in South Africa'.[24] In addition to reaffirming support both for the UN mandatory arms embargo against South Africa and for the Commonwealth Gleneagles Declaration of 1977 which discouraged all sporting contacts with South Africa, certain new measures were agreed upon. These included a ban on new government-to-government loans; unilateral action to preclude the import of Krugerrands where this is possible; a ban on government funding for trade missions to South Africa; embargoes on the sale and export of oil, nuclear goods, materiel and technology, and on the sale of computer equipment capable of use by South African police or military; an embargo on imports of arms, ammunition, military vehicles and paramilitary equipment from South Africa, and a ban on all military co-operation with South Africa.[25]

The Commonwealth Heads of Government also decided to appoint a group of eminent persons to initiate a dialogue with the South African government and to review the situation in six months' time. It was announced that if progress had not been made in dismantling apartheid within a reasonable period, further steps could be considered, including a ban on air links, investment and tourism.[26]

It is impossible to predict future developments in respect of sanctions at the UN. The persistent record of condemnation and the initiation of punitive measures by western powers, however mild these measures appear to be, have certainly undermined any vestige of international legitimacy for the system of apartheid and further international action can not be ruled out. South Africa's vulnerability to international sanctions and the policy dilemmas it poses for western governments are discussed in Chapter 9.

5 Sanctions in Regional Settings

Chapters 3 and 4 gave a brief account of the sanctions record of the League and the United Nations; this chapter reviews the major cases of sanctions which have been applied in regional settings. These include the organisationally-sponsored sanctions imposed in the Western hemisphere by the Organisation of American States (OAS) against the Dominican Republic and Cuba and in the Middle East by the Arab League against Egypt. Soviet bloc action against East European governments who have failed to toe the Kremlin line is also discussed in this chapter. Although there is no exact Eastern European counterpart to the OAS – the Warsaw Pact, like NATO, is a security treaty under Article 51 of the UN Charter and not a regional body under Chapter VIII – it provides a framework for collective action. And the cohesion of the Soviet bloc has also been reinforced by the Cominform (dissolved in 1949), the Council for Mutual Economic Assistance (CMEA or COMECON)[1] and regular congresses of communist parties.

(a) Sanctions in Eastern Europe

Measures imposed by the Soviet bloc on Yugoslavia and Albania may be considered as regional sanctions in terms of the definition set out in Chapter 1. That is to say, they were penalties for behaviour which in Soviet eyes was unacceptably non-conformist in respect of bloc norms. These norms challenge the right of governments of individual states in Eastern Europe to determine their own internal and external policies on lines which deviate from those approved by Moscow. Such deviation is perceived as a threat to regional stability and security.

Yugoslavia's independent policy made it the first target of Soviet anger in 1948. As James Barber notes 'Tito challenged Stalin's expectations of a disciplined subordination to the Soviet Union; to have ignored [his] actions would have jeopardized

53

the *whole structure* by encouraging others to display a similar independence.'[2] The campaign of ostracism designed to discredit Tito's government included the severance of diplomatic and economic links and a full-scale propaganda war. Yugoslavia was expelled from the Cominform; trade ceased; debts were not settled; borders were closed.[3]

The economic embargo was a severe blow for the Yugoslav economy which was struggling to recover from the Second World War. Success for the first Five Year Plan depended on the flow of Soviet aid, technical assistance, and capital goods supplied on easy credit terms. At the time of the break, one-half of Yugoslavia's external trade was with the bloc, while trade with Western Europe was negligible. Survival required a drastic reorientation of trade towards Western Europe and massive injections of aid. Both of these occurred. Between 1950 and 1954 $1 billion of western aid was made available[4] and by 1952 19.3 per cent of Yugoslav imports came from the United States and 20.3 per cent from West Germany, while 14.7 per cent of exports went to the former and 23.7 per cent to the latter. Normalisation of relations with the USSR came in 1955, two years after Stalin's death, but there was no return to the bloc. Yugoslavia continued to pursue its own brand of communism and in foreign policy espoused a policy of non-alignment between east and west. One effect of Soviet bloc pressure was to reinforce strong feelings of popular loyalty to Tito, a charismatic leader with a record of heroic resistance to Nazi Germany.

The next target of Soviet wrath was Albania which 'defected' to the Chinese communist camp in 1961. This time there was no full-scale boycott, but the USSR led a programme of denial which suspended credits, withdrew exports and cut back on trade.[5] Again, as in the case of Yugoslavia, reorientation of trade and new sources of external aid were needed and the People's Republic of China (PRC) became Albania's friend in need. Agreements for increased Sino–Albanian trade were signed in January 1962; thereafter China became the main source of loans. With this support and a drive for self-sufficiency the Albanian economy did reasonably well in the 1960s; but in the 1970s a deterioration in relations with the PRC left Albania very isolated and on bad terms with both major communist powers. It had ceased to subscribe to or participate in COM-ECON in 1962.

Both Yugoslavia and Albania were therefore successful in establishing autonomy outside the Soviet sphere of influence despite political and economic pressure. Hungary and Czechoslovakia were to be less fortunate: in both cases, military coercion was used to keep them within its bounds.

In 1956, in the midst of internal turmoil and with Soviet troops in Budapest at the invitation of the previous leader, Hungarian Prime Minister Imre Nagy tried to democratise the political system and leave the Warsaw Pact. No help was forthcoming from the West and Hungarian aspirations were brutally crushed by Soviet forces. Twelve years later Czechoslovakia under the leadership of Alexander Dubcek tried to establish a new kind of communist system – 'with a human face' – and despite strenuous assertions of loyalty to the Warsaw Pact it too suffered crushing military intervention. On this occasion, contingents from all other Warsaw Pact countries except Romania took part. In fact, the East German government was one of the main proponents of armed intervention.

Shortly after the invasion of Czechoslovakia in August 1968, the so-called Brezhnev doctrine made its appearance, first as an article in *Pravda* and later in speeches by the Soviet Foreign Minister and by Brezhnev himself.[6] The nub of the doctrine was the right of fraternal intervention in any communist state which was in danger from internal or external forces hostile to 'socialism'; it therefore sought to confirm norms which were applicable to all socialist (communist) states and to justify military action in support of these norms. Clearly such action is inconsistent with the UN Charter which is founded on principles of sovereignty and non-intervention, bans the use of force except in self-defence and permits no 'higher law'. But the absence of any effective authority at the UN level means that hegemonial powers enjoy great freedom in controlling their respective spheres; and as Franck and Weisband have pointed out there are similarities in the regional 'doctrines' propounded by both superpowers.[7] Central America and Eastern Europe are spheres of influence not in the nineteenth-century mode of colonial appendages, acknowledged to be non-self-governing, but in the contemporary mode of nominally independent states which have some opportunities to make political and economic connections outside the 'sphere' but are basically subject to a set of norms spelled out and enforced to varying degrees by the hegemonial power. Even if they 'escape', they may continue to suffer 'punishment' and attempts by the hegemon to re-establish 'authority'.

For each superpower, the ideology and perceived hostility of the other provides a demonology against which 'virtue' can be mobilised: capitalism or communism is upheld as the morally superior system. In this situation, where offenders violate prevailing norms, the term sanction must probably be accepted as a description of non-violent, conformity-defending measures, although it carries no connotations of legitimacy for the system or its rules. It is to be expected that the right of the leading power to organise punishment will be contested by the target (where this is feasible), by the opposing camp, and possibly by other governments as well and it is to be hoped that military intervention which clearly violates Charter rules does not acquire a sanctions label as this would make nonsense of the term.

SANCTIONS IN THE WESTERN HEMISPHERE

The Soviet Union invented the Brezhnev doctrine which obviously conflicts with international law. Earlier, the US had argued that the naval 'quarantine' of Cuba during the 1962 missile crisis was not 'enforcement action' which would have required Security Council authorisation, but collective action in defence of the peace and security of the Americas.[8] It was noted in Chapter 2 that the OAS Charter enshrines the principle of non-intervention while its security arm, the Rio Treaty, provides for collective self defence. But among OAS members, interpretations differ on the scope of these provisions. The United States accepts and upholds the norm of non-intervention in respect of extra-hemisphere influence and penetration, but excludes its own activities, whereas for other members of the organisation it is the United States which is the most likely source of unwelcome intervention. Where the majority of OAS members sought to preserve the status quo, there was a convergence of objectives but for the United States since the onset of the Cold War 'acceptable' political stability in Latin America means non-communist governments; regimes ideologically linked with and financially supported by the Soviet Union are unacceptable. In other words, the United States has set its own standard of regional legitimacy which is not shared by all other OAS members, and in pursuing its own goal of upholding this standard it has become increasingly isolated from them.

The progressively widening gap between the US and the rest of the OAS has been demonstrated in open disagreement over appropriate postures and policies in the Falklands dispute and towards the internal situation in both Grenada and Nicaragua. The Falklands conflict is discussed in some detail in Chapter 6. In the case of Grenada in 1983, the US intervened militarily after the violent overthrow of the Grenadan government, responding to appeals from the beleaguered Governor-General and members of the Organisation of East Caribbean States (OECS) of which it is obviously not a member. There was no recourse to the OAS and the use of force ran into strong opposition from the majority of its members who voted to condemn the intervention in the UN General Assembly.[9] Nicaragua is perceived by the Reagan Administration as following the Cuban path: alignment with the Soviet Union and destabilisation of Central America. As such, it is said to be violating regional norms and threatening the peace and security of the hemisphere. Again this view is not shared by the rest of the OAS. Unilateral measures taken by the US include a total trade embargo and other economic measures which could (and have been) called sanctions; aid to the rebel 'Contras' who are fighting the Sandinista government, and CIA sponsored activities which led Nicaragua to ask the International Court of Justice to order provisional measures under Article 41 of its Statute which would bring all military and para-military activities by the United States to an end.[10]

In the early 1960s however, there was more OAS support for US policies, as illustrated by the cases of the Dominican Republic and Cuba.

(a) The Dominican Republic

Economic sanctions were first invoked by the OAS in August 1960 when the Foreign Ministers of member states meeting in Costa Rica, condemned the Trujillo regime in the Dominican

Republic for committing acts of aggression and intervention in Venezuela and for implication in the attempted assassination of the Venezuelan president. Acting in terms of Articles 6 and 8 of the Rio Treaty, the Foreign Ministers passed a unanimous resolution which called for the breaking of diplomatic relations between all members of the OAS and the Dominican Republic, the partial interruption of economic relations, and the immediate suspension of trade in arms and implements of war of every kind. The extension of embargoes to cover trade in other articles was to be studied, and the Security Council informed of OAS action. It was agreed that the measures would be discontinued when the government of the Dominican Republic ceased to constitute a danger to the peace and security of the hemisphere.

There was a division of opinion in the Security Council as to whether the OAS had acted improperly in not seeking prior authorisation for its action, a point of view supported by the Soviet Union but opposed by the United States. The matter was left unresolved; the Security Council merely acknowledged receipt of the information from the Secretary-General of the OAS and noted the application of sanctions on a regional basis. The Soviet Union and Poland abstained from voting.

In January 1961 the Council of the OAS voted fourteen to one, with six abstentions, that it would be feasible to extend the embargo to include trade in petroleum and petroleum products, trucks and spare parts. Cuba voted in favour. The United States also penalised imports of sugar from the Dominican Republic by imposing an entry fee of two cents a pound, payable in advance, and later prohibited the distribution to the Dominican Republic of part of the former Cuban quota.

In the course of 1961 Trujillo was assassinated and a more democratic regime installed. OAS sanctions were removed in January 1962 and the United States immediately extended an emergency credit of $25 million.

The Dominican Republic as the small client of a superpower, with no outside support, offered the elements of a classic case for the application of external economic pressure. It is a leading supplier of sugar; nine-tenths of the crop is exported, and although coffee and cocoa are important exports, sugar accounts for over 50 per cent of the total value of exports. But the period in which sanctions were operating was too short to isolate their economic effects, and in any case the embargoes were limited in scope and not wholly observed. Some effects on trade were discernible: exports of unrefined sugar which were worth $80.1 million in 1960 were only $59.8 million in 1961; by 1963 they had recovered to $88.8 million.[11] Anna Schreiber notes that the 'primary economic effect of US sugar restrictions had been to prevent a large increase in Dominican revenues at a time when this could have substantially bolstered the troubled economy'.[12]

Politically the effects of concerted condemnation and pressure by twenty nations in the hemisphere may have assisted internal resistance and helped to bring the downfall of Trujillo and his regime. More important, perhaps, was the accompaniment of economic coercion by military threats and intensive diplomatic pressure from the US, alongside CIA involvement in Dominican politics. The absence of ideological overtones and the general unpopularity of the regime inside and outside the Dominican Republic simplified the issues in this case,[13]

It will be recalled that the later course of United States relations with the Dominican Republic was far from smooth. Initially, American military intervention in the Dominican Republic in 1965 was not undertaken with the support of the OAS, and indeed was strongly opposed by a number of members, particularly Chile, Ecuador, Mexico, Peru and Uruguay.

(b) Cuba

In the case of Cuba sanctions were to be harsher and more prolonged. The United States imposed unilateral embargoes in August 1960 – less than a year after Fidel Castro came to power – and by October it had banned all exports (with the exception of medicine and food) and reduced the sugar quota to zero. Diplomatic relations were severed in January 1961. These steps followed Cuban expropriation without compensation of American property valued by the US Department of Commerce at $1000 million and the imposition of discriminatory taxes and licences on American products.

All trade between the United States and Cuba (except medicine and food) was embargoed early in 1962, and the sale, charter and transfer of ships to the Cuban government and its nationals were prohibited without official approval. Normal communication links by sea and air were also severed although an airlift of Cuban refugees continued. In the interim, however, there had been the abortive Bay of Pigs invasion and recourse to the OAS for support for United States action.

The United States tried to raise the Cuban issue at the OAS meeting at San José in August 1960, but was unable to obtain more than a general declaration rejecting any extra-continental intervention or Sino–Soviet meddling in Latin America. During 1961, however, Castro publicly acknowledged his Marxist–Leninist affiliation and spoke of the Cuban revolution as a socialist, anti-imperialist movement. This posture enabled the United States to achieve stronger OAS support and at the eighth meeting of the OAS Organ of Consultation held at Punta Del Este in January 1962, adherence by any member of the OAS to Marxist–Leninist ideology was declared to be incompatible with the inter-American system. Only Cuba voted against the resolution. There being no provision for expulsion of members in the Bogota Charter, Cuba was declared to have placed herself 'voluntarily' outside the system (by a bare two-thirds majority of votes) and it was also resolved to suspend immediately trade with Cuba in arms and implements of war of every kind (16 votes in favour and 4 abstentions). The suspension of trade in other items was to be studied further.[14]

Cuba appealed to the Security Council and in March 1962 proposed that an Advisory Opinion should be sought from the International Court of Justice on questions relating to sanctions, claiming that the OAS measures should be suspended in the meantime. This suggestion was not taken up. In the Security Council debate, the United States asserted the OAS right to take any action without being hampered by the veto.

The development of the missile crisis in October 1962 brought temporary unanimity in the OAS on the dangers of Castro's alignment with the Soviet Union. The United States was able to obtain unanimous OAS support on 23 October for a naval 'quarantine' (announced the previous day) to prevent delivery of weapons to Cuba, and a resolution passed by the OAS Council, acting provisionally as the Organ of Consultation under the Rio Treaty, authorised members to take all measures individually and collectively, including the use of armed force, to ensure hemispheric security. Although the United States took the major responsibility for the blockade against the shipment of offensive weapons to Cuba, other OAS members offered or contributed ships, bases and troops in support. The Security Council considered the matter on the same day, at the request of both the United States and Cuban governments, but took no action. The missile crisis was settled directly between the United States and the Soviet Union; the quarantine, effective from 24 October, was lifted on 20 November.[15]

The discovery of a cache of arms of Cuban origin in Venezuela early in 1964 led to further accusations of Cuban subversion and in July 1964, at the ninth meeting of the Organ of Consultation of the OAS, both Venezuela and the United States called for mandatory sanctions. Action was taken in accordance with the relevant articles of the Rio Treaty: all diplomatic relations were to be severed; all trade except food, medicine, and medical equipment was to be banned; no sea transport was to be permitted except for humanitarian reasons. Cuba was warned that persistence in 'aggression' might lead to resort to force in self-defence. But Chile, Bolivia and Uruguay dissented from these recommendations, and Mexico did not comply with the decision to sever diplomatic relations.

In the meantime the United States continued its unilateral pressure on Cuba. In July 1963 all Cuban assets in United States banks had been frozen and all transactions concerning property with a Cuban interest had been placed under licence. The United States government also campaigned very actively for support from its western allies to isolate Cuba from the so-called 'free-world'. This attempt was not wholly successful.[16] Canada's reaction was typical of the rest; embargoes were placed on strategic items which would contribute to Cuba's military strength, but normal trade continued.

The OAS sanctions front was crumbling by the time sanctions were officially lifted in 1975. Chile resumed trade with Cuba early in 1970 and Argentina in 1974. However, the United States still maintains its unilateral measures, and bilateral relations between the two countries, have showed few signs of improving, particularly over the last decade. Cuba is viewed by the Reagan Administration as a Soviet puppet with a record of extra-hemispheric adventurism (giving military assistance as a Soviet proxy to radical governments and liberation movements in Africa) and intra-hemispheric subversion and revolution (as shown by assistance to the ill-fated Bishop government in Grenada, the rebel movement in El Salvador and the Sandinista government in Nicaragua). Particularly in its inter-American policies, Cuba is regarded by the US government as an alien system, infecting the area with poison, but this attitude is not shared by other governments in the region.

It is obviously extremely difficult to make any evaluation of the impact of the OAS sanctions on the Cuban economy. Not only have US measures remained in force, and the United States was, of course, the dominant economic influence prior to the 1960s, but Cuba itself has experienced a political, social and economic revolution over the past 25 years. Moreover, Soviet assistance has been forthcoming on a consistently massive scale.

Sugar was the key commodity: the chief export crop and the mainstay of the economy. Under Castro, sugar estates were expropriated and collective farms established. The United States had formerly bought approximately three million tons of sugar per year, one half of the total crop, and the reduction of the US sugar quota to zero forced a drastic reorientation of Cuba's foreign trade. Schreiber notes that '[B]ecause Cuba deliberately sought to end its trade dependence on the United States, some trade reorientation would have occurred even if the US had not applied economic coercion, but the trade boycott made the break more complete than it would otherwise have been.[17]

Out of total export earnings of $617.3 million in 1960, sugar contributed $467.5 million (over 75 per cent) while tobacco and tobacco manufactures, the next most important foreign exchange earners, contributed only $63.0 million.[18] Unless sugar could be exported, imports, which accounted for 35 per cent of the gross national product in 1959, could not be financed. Import control was established in 1959 and consumer goods imports declined by 44 per cent in value between 1957 and 1962. But Cuba depended on imported energy, and capital goods were essential not only for industrial development but also for re-equipment of US supplied infrastructure for which parts were no longer available.

Trade with the rest of Latin America declined, but except for the loss of imports of petroleum from Venezuela, this was not of such vital significance to Cuba. As Schreiber points out, '... OAS action was more a symbolic form of cooperation with the United States than an effective way of injuring Cuba.'[19] After 1963 trade with Western Europe and Canada increased, and there was some growth in trade with Japan, Egypt and Morocco, but the leading support role was played by the Soviet Union and other Communist countries which supplied the goods Cuba needed and provided the credits required to finance their import.

In the three years from 1959 to 1962, the dominant position of the United States in Cuba's external trade was eliminated. Whereas in 1959 the United States supplied 68 per cent of Cuban imports and took 69 per cent of Cuban exports, by 1962 Cuban trade with the United States was negligible; 82 per cent of Cuba's export trade and 85 per cent of her import trade was conducted with Communist countries, particularly the Soviet Union, Czechoslovakia and mainland China. As early as February 1960, under the terms of a bilateral trade agreement, the Soviet government agreed to buy 2.7 million tons of sugar and to increase purchases if the United States placed a total embargo on imports of sugar from Cuba. A long-term credit of $100 million was also extended. A long-term trade agreement concluded in 1963 provided for Soviet imports of sugar to increase by one million tons a year to a maximum of five million tons in 1968; imports would be maintained at that level until 1970. The price was fixed at 6c (US) per lb – lower than the ruling market price, but offering stability in earnings. There was also considerable expansion of the Soviet merchant fleet to handle Cuban trade; this was necessary because the US operated a blacklist of shipowners whose vessels carried cargoes to Cuba; no US government cargoes or government-financed cargoes could be carried in their ships, and western allies were quite co-operative over the shipping embargo.

But in spite of this considerable Soviet support, supplemented by aid from other Communist countries in Europe and from the People's Republic of China, the Cuban economy experienced serious difficulties, particularly in the period 1961–4 which was when the embargoes had their main impact.[20] For instance, the US embargoes had an immediate effect on Cuba's port system, which was not equipped with facilities for handling ocean-borne freight nor with adequate storage facilities.[21] An effort to break the traditional dependence on sugar led to an unwise diversification of productive activity and squandering of capital between 1961 and 1963. From 1964 to 1970 Cuba came to depend even more heavily on Soviet economic aid and preferential trade arrangements,[22] and a swing to over-emphasis on agriculture with an unrealistic target of 10 million tons of sugar production in 1970 followed the earlier over-emphasis on industrialisation. Commentators have concluded that the overall growth of the Cuban economy during the first ten years of revolution was almost nil, although redistribution of wealth brought greater social equality.[23] Throughout the 1960s Cuba ran an annual deficit with the Soviet Union which was never less than $100 million and at times nearly three times as high.[24] To reduce Cuban dependence on imported oil, the USSR assisted with the construction of a a nuclear power station, and in recent years there have been marked improvements in industrial and agricultural production and productivity, but dependence on the USSR is still very heavy. In 1980, for instance, Cuba received $3000 million in Soviet aid as well as arms deliveries; the USSR bought sugar at 42 per cent over the world price and supplied Cuba with oil at prices 40 per cent below those of OPEC.

There can certainly be no doubt that the United States policy of economic denial, which for a decade was also supported by the OAS, has increased the cost to the Soviet Union of maintaining a communist outpost in the western hemisphere, thus fulfilling one of the stated goals of the Kennedy Administration and all successive Administrations.[25] It has presumably also retarded Cuba's economic development in some respects although it has been argued that dependence on the USSR is less restrictive of diversification of the Cuban economy than the former dependence on the US.[26]

But once the OAS support was removed, the US measures became no more than an extension of its Cold War policies towards the USSR and other communist countries. Here one enters a 'grey' area of continuing economic warfare – the use of foreign policy weapons which make things difficult for the target but are not related to specific acts of wrong-doing. The Cuban political system is seen as a continuing affront to the capitalist world which surrounds it; it is in the enemy camp, and is treated as an enemy.

In the 1980s the US can no longer rely on the OAS and so the convenience, or advantage, of having a regional organisation to legitimise its policies has been lost; it faces the prospect of acting not only without OAS support but with its open condemnation (as over Grenada).

Rule making and rule enforcement by hegemonial powers is an important issue which is taken up in the final chapter; this chapter concludes with a short account of Arab League measures against Egypt which followed the signing of the Camp David accords in 1978 and the subsequent Israeli–Egyptian peace treaty in March 1979.

SANCTIONS IN THE ARAB WORLD

Arab boycotts of Israel and Israel's friends, allies and business partners do not qualify as sanctions in terms of our definition and are therefore not dealt with in detail in this chapter or elsewhere in the book, except as illustration of the effects of economic coercion. Israel is not a member of any Arab organisation; nor can it be required to conform to Arab norms. From the outset the Arab position which denies that Israel has a right to exist has been legally untenable, given that the United Nations admitted Israel to full membership in 1948. Since the Six Day War of 1967, the question of recognition of Israel has been linked by Arab governments to Israel's recognition of the right of the Palestinians to self-determination. The economic measures applied by Arab states to Israel and to Israel's friends and allies in the continuing cold – and occasionally hot – war waged in the Middle East must be categorised as economic warfare; as such they have exceeded the bounds of legality in some cases. For instance in preventing Israel from using the Suez Canal Egypt contravened the 1888 Constantinople Convention and was censured by the Security Council (Resolution S/2241, 1 September 1951); as well, the discriminatory oil embargoes imposed on some industrialised countries by the Arab members of OPEC in 1973–4 were questionable in terms of obligations under the General Agreement on Tariffs and Trade (GATT) and under bilateral treaties between certain producer countries and the United States.[27] Likewise, Israel's policy of settlement and even annexation of occupied territories has not been consistent with international law[28] and acts such as the bombing of the Iraqui nuclear reactor in 1981, the invasion of Lebanon in 1982, and the bombing of the head-quarters of the Palestine Liberation Organisation in Tunis in October 1985 stretch the concepts of self-defence and reprisal far beyond reasonable limits. Indeed, the bombing of Tunisia prompted a Security Council resolution condemning 'the act of armed aggression perpetrated by Israel ... in flagrant violation of the Charter of the United Nations, international law and norms of conduct' (Resolution 573, 4 October 1985). This resolution was adopted by 14 votes with one abstention – the United States. Mention of sanctions in the resolution would have ensured its veto by the United States which can obviously prevent any Security Council action to recommend or order sanctions against Israel, including suspension or expulsion. The General Assembly, on the other hand, reflecting the Third World majority, has tended to place Israel in a 'pariah' category similar to that of South Africa. The adoption of Resolution 3379 on 10 November 1975 which equated Zionism with racism did much to discredit the Assembly in the eyes of the United States and Arab efforts to have Israel barred from UN bodies have failed in the face of strong US opposition, buttressed with threats to withdraw financial support if such resolutions were carried.

It is, of course, arguable that where Security Council condemnation is on record, as in Resolution 573, UN members, as well as Tunisia itself, would be free to impose voluntary sanctions against Israel for its breach of international law. This, after all, is what the United States expected its allies to do in the case of Iran. If such action had been taken against Israel it would be a case for the next chapter which deals with sanctions adopted outside organisational frameworks. The issue of relevance here is the effort by the League of Arab States to discipline Egypt – a leading member of the organisation – for its recognition of Israel and conclusion of a peace treaty with it in 1979. This act dealt a profound blow to Arab solidarity and set Egypt at odds with all other Arab governments. The Arab League claimed that it directly contravened the ban on separate agreements with Israel affirmed at the League summit in Rabat in 1974.

Radical members of the League – Algeria, Iraq, Libya, Syria and the Palestine Liberation Organisation (PLO) – wanted sanctions against Egypt after Camp David; once the Peace Treaty had been signed they were quickly able to convince the moderates, led by Saudi-Arabia, that Egypt must be isolated. At a ministerial meeting held in Baghdad from 27 to 31 March 1979, a very comprehensive set of diplomatic and economic measures was imposed. Victor Lavy notes that the 'clear message of the ... summit was that Egypt no longer belonged to the family of the Arab world'.[29]

Diplomatic isolation was to be achieved by suspension of Egypt's membership in the Arab League and affiliated organisations. The League's Headquarters was moved from Cairo to Tunis and UN regional offices for the Arab region were also to be moved out of Egypt. Arab governments withdrew their ambassadors from Cairo. In the economic sphere, the sale of oil and oil products to Egypt was banned; all aid to Egypt from Arab funds, banks and financial institutions was to be halted; no financial transactions would be allowed between the Egyptian government and other Arab governments. But exchange control was not instituted, Arab funds were not withdrawn from Egyptian financial institutions and there was no mention of the 'oil weapon' being used against Egypt's 'friends'. The Baghdad communiqué stressed continued co-operation with the 'fraternal Egyptian people' – in contrast to the unfraternal government of Anwar Sadat. The intention was obviously to discredit Sadat's policies, emphasising that they were a betrayal of Arab and Palestinian interests.

Egypt was also suspended from other Middle Eastern organisations, notably the Arab Monetary Fund, the Islamic Conference and OAPEC. The Gulf Organisation for Development in Egypt (GODE) financed by Kuwait, Qatar and Saudi Arabia was dissolved and the Arab Organisation for Military Industrialisation (AOMI) was also closed down in July 1979. It had used Gulf money and Egyptian labour and technology to manufacture weapons. By the end of 1979 official Arab aid to Egypt had ceased to flow. Sadat estimated it at $600 million; other estimates varied from $750 million to $1000 million. Most of it came from Saudi Arabia.

It has been suggested that the economic effects of the sanctions were exaggerated by President Sadat in order to get western aid[30] and in strictly economic terms there do not seem to have been dramatically adverse effects. Financial and military aid was forthcoming from the west, particularly the United States; tourism, a significant foreign exchange earner, was not affected, nor were annual remittances of approximately $2 billion from approximately one million migrant Egyptian workers in other Arab countries. There was some effect on Egypt's trade with Arab countries (which was limited in any case) particularly where substitutes for Egyptian products were available; Lavy points out that in other cases, such as high quality Egyptian cotton, exports actually increased.[31] Egypt had the revenue from the Suez Canal tolls and was self-sufficient in oil. Furthermore there were obvious offsetting benefits in trade with Israel which was estimated to be worth $111 million annually.[32]

As would be expected, the Sadat government did not accept Arab League sanctions meekly. It challenged the legality of the Baghdad meeting (which was not a regular meeting) and questioned its decisions because they were not unanimous. This is reminiscent of Italy's challenge to League Council decisions, but obviously if unanimity is needed, neither condemnation nor penalties could ever be obtained in an international body.

Egypt declared the sanctions to be 'null and void', having 'frozen' its membership of the Arab League prior to suspension. This involved the withholding of dues and participation. Local assets of Arab organisations, including those of the Arab League, were also frozen.[33]

The diplomatic boycott of Egypt was beginning to show some signs of thaw as early as mid-1980; Saudi Arabia was very uneasy about the revival of Islamic fundamentalism, and the Iran–Iraq war gave Egypt a chance to sell arms to Iraq. Concern about Libya in Sudan and elsewhere focused attention again on the possible utility of Egypt's large standing army, and full diplomatic relations were resumed between the Egyptian and Sudanese governments in the summer of 1981. Sadat's assassination in October of that year brought Hosni Mubarak to power in Egypt and as he had not been personally identified with the Camp David process it was easier for him to initiate normalisation of relations with Arab countries. The non-aligned movement had never acted formally on the Baghdad summit's recommendation to suspend Egypt: Mubarak visited New Delhi in February 1983 and a conference of non-aligned journalists took place in Cairo in the following year. In 1984 diplomatic relations with Jordan were re-established, there was agreement in principle to restore diplomatic relations with Morocco, and the Islamic Conference summit held in January invited Egypt to resume membership. But Egypt was still excluded from the Arab League in 1985 and did not attend the Casablanca summit in August of that year.

It is impossible to say whether Arab League sanctions were conducive to Sadat's murder; they obviously did not serve to enhance his standing in the Arab world, but external condemnation may have helped to solidify support for the peace treaty inside Egypt. The period when diplomatic isolation was at its peak was certainly anomalous; Egypt has traditionally exercised leadership in the Arab world and, under Nasser, took a strong anti-imperialist, pro-Third World stance. For Egypt to be a 'pariah' – outside the Arab family – was a very strange situation, and one which would not be expected to last for very long given Egypt's key role in the Middle East as well as the propensity for discord and violence within the Arab world as a whole which has been amply demonstrated in recent years.

6 Sanctions outside Organisational Frameworks

Since 1979 there has been a sharp deterioration in East–West relations which has brought heightened anxiety about the possibility of a third world war. There have been several well-publicised cases of sanctions during this period, most of them linked to East–West hostility and all of them marked by discord and acrimony among the sanctioning group. One of the sharpest controversies developed within the western alliance when the United States attempted to block further construction of the gas pipeline from Siberia to West Germany as part of a set of penalties designed to punish the Soviet Union for its role in the Polish crisis.

The problems of organising collective sanctions are hard enough to resolve within an organisational framework where some procedures for discussion and decision making are already in place and some ground rules exist for determining when and what penalties should be imposed; they are compounded when *ad hoc* coalitions come together to try and organise a group effort. In this chapter, following the pattern of Chapters 3, 4 and 5, brief accounts will be given of experience with sanctions against Iran in the hostages crisis; against the USSR following its military intervention in Afghanistan; against the USSR and Poland following the imposition of martial law in Poland; and against Argentina in the Falklands crisis.

THE TEHRAN HOSTAGES CRISIS

The seizure of the United States embassy and 52 hostages, (mainly US diplomatic personnel) by Iranian militants on 4 November 1979 ushered in 14 months of intensive and varied efforts to persuade the Iranian government to release the Americans unharmed. Success did not come until 20 January 1981, the day of President Reagan's inauguration; the intervening period had produced diplomatic negotiations, recourse to the UN and the International Court of Justice (ICJ), punitive measures against Iran, an abortive rescue attempt by the United States, and threats by Iran to put the hostages on trial. Throughout this period Iran was in the throes of revolutionary upheaval while in the United States President Carter's political fortunes worsened dramatically.

The norm violation in the hostages case was never in doubt. Neither Iran's objection to the admission of the Shah to the United States for medical treatment and the Administration's refusal to send him back to Iran to stand trial, nor the Iranian government's accusations of prior and prolonged US wrongdoing which were transmitted to the ICJ[1] could justify the serious breach of time-honoured international law regarding the immunity of diplomatic personnel and property and the obligation of a host government to protect them.[2]

The United States took the case to the Security Council which on 4 December, in a rare display of unanimity, called for the release of the hostages. Resolution 457 described the situation as 'one which could have grave consequences for international peace and security'. At a subsequent meeting on 31 December the Council noted the opinion of the Secretary-General that the crisis did threaten international peace and security, and threatened 'effective measures' (under Chapter VII of the Charter) if Iran continued to defy the Council (Resolution 461). The United States also took its case to the World Court seeking interim measures of protection and a judgement on the merits of the case. In an Order for Provisional Measures issued on 15 December the Court called for the release of the hostages, restoration of their diplomatic privileges and the restoration of the Embassy. Both the United States and Iran were advised to do nothing which would aggravate the situation.[3].

Iran failed to comply with any of these calls and a visit to Tehran by the UN Secretary-General proved fruitless. The Ayatollah Khomeini refused to meet him and he was not allowed to see the hostages. On 10 January 1980 the United States sought a Security Council order for mandatory economic sanctions but this was vetoed by the USSR on 13 January. The Soviet Union had abstained on Resolution 461, claiming that the issue was a bilateral one between the United States and Iran.[4]

Failure to obtain either the release of the hostages or a UN sanctions order meant that the United States would have to take unilateral measures and hope to associate other governments with its action. Given the injury it had suffered, some self-help response by the US was to be expected; the question was what steps it would take, and whether its allies would join in. Between November 1979 and April 1980 the Carter Administration progressively adopted a series of penalties which included the freezing of assets of the Iranian state and their listing with a view to possible confiscation to meet claims of US nationals against Iran; a ban on imports of petroleum from Iran and later on all trade with Iran (except food and medicine); investigation of Iranian students in the US (and subsequent deportation of those whose visas were not in order) and cancellation of visas for Iranians to enter the US; a ban on travel to Iran for US citizens; a ban on financial dealings between Americans and Iran, and the severance of diplomatic relations.[5] Schachter points out that these non-military measures 'were generally regarded as permissible self-help under international law ... *vis-à-vis* Iran'.[6]

If there had been no veto of the US draft resolution in the Security Council, sanctions would have been mandatory for UN members. As it was, the record of the Security Council and ICJ amounted to no more than authoritative pronouncements of wrong-doing. The veto in this case underlines the near impossibility of achieving UN 'enforcement'. It is incontrovertible that the protection of diplomats is of basic importance to the conduct of inter-state relations, irrespective of enmities or friendships. But was the detention of 52 US diplomats a threat to international peace and security? And would international sanctions be the best way to remove that threat and free the hostages? Or would they 'aggravate the situation', which the ICJ had expressed advised against? Neither Third World nor Western countries subscribed to the Soviet view that only bilateral issues were involved; clearly a general principle was at stake. But the USSR was not the only government to baulk at sanctions. Third World countries were not willing to discipline Iran and even Western governments were loath to join the US in applying sanctions. There was concern abut contributing to a worsening of the internal situation in Iran; there was also traditional reluctance to interfere with normal commercial and financial relationships on political grounds. Moreover, the Soviet invasion of Afghanistan occurred in December 1979 and thereafter the Western allies were faced with two crises to which the United States expected them to respond, the second being more generally alarming than the first. And the dangers of alienating all of Islam by punishing Iran at a time when it could be a useful bulwark against the Soviet Union and communism were not overlooked.

The rescue attempt which failed so dramatically and disastrously on 24 April 1980 did not help the Carter Administration domestically or internationally. Not only was its image of competence seriously damaged, but the propriety of resorting to such action just before the World Court's final judgement was due to be handed down was open to question. The Court itself had dealt with most of the issues involved in its Provisional Order; in the judgement dated 24 May 1980 it also recognised that the US could claim compensation from Iran. Its comment on the rescue attempt was that it ignored the order of 15 December not to aggravate tension and was not compatible with 'respect for the judicial process'.[7]

The abortive rescue attempt may also have discouraged allies of the United States from imposing severe economic sanctions.[8] In May, under heavy US pressure, the members of the European Community (EC) and certain other Western industrialised countries imposed limited restrictions on trade with Iran. EC members banned exports to Iran under contracts signed after 4 November 1979 but the British ban was not retroactive, taking effect on 29 May and exempting not only existing contracts but also extensions of existing contracts. Australia, Canada, Japan and Norway followed the EC line.

The United States lifted its sanctions immediately after the signing of agreements to end the crisis in Tehran and Algiers on 19 January 1981. The Foreign Ministers of the EC removed their trade sanctions the following day and other countries followed suit. In terms of the agreements reached between the US and Iran, Iranian assets were unfrozen and returned to Iran via the Bank of England and the Central Bank of Algiers, except that some funds were to be returned to New York or held in London to repay outstanding Iranian bank loans, and a security account of $1000 million was to be established in London for the settlement of claims.

Assessment of the effect of the sanctions imposed on Iran by the United States and its allies is very difficult. As in all cases of sanctions there were many other factors influencing the course of events whose impact cannot be disentangled. In Iran itself a violent revolution was in progress. Moreover, the commercial sanctions imposed by western countries were only in effect for eight months and although participants represented a powerful economic group of states, they were limited in number and were less than eager to sever commercial links with Iran. Japan is on record as buying oil from Iran which had been destined for the United States, and this obviously weakened the impact of the US oil embargo.[9]

It has been convincingly argued, particularly by Robert Carswell, that the financial sanctions imposed by the United States did have an effect over the long period.[10] Twelve billion dollars of assets were frozen and Iran needed funds to finance the war with Iraq which began in the autumn of 1980. He comments that the 'sanctions undoubtedly caused Iran difficulties, but probably not insuperable ones'.[11] But it is not unfair to speculate that the open reluctance of the allies to support the US, and the disinclination of any wider group of countries to join in sanctions gave some comfort to the Iranian authorities. It may also be suggested that one of the factors influencing the eventual agreement to release the hostages was the fact that the last ounce of publicity had been squeezed out of their captivity. There may also have been concern that the incoming Reagan Administration would be less hesitant to take more drastic action.

THE SOVIET INTERVENTION IN AFGHANISTAN

In late December 1979 in an action widely condemned by the international community, the Soviet government sent some 85 000 troops into Afghanistan. The justification that the Afghan government, which had been pro-Moscow since a coup in April 1978, had requested Soviet help because of external threats from the United States, China and Pakistan, was hardly convincing, particularly as a new head of government was promptly installed in Kabul.

The Soviet Union was able to block any condemnation of its action in the Security Council but outraged Third World countries called an Emergency Session of the General Assembly under the Uniting for Peace Resolution and sponsored a resolution calling for the complete withdrawal of all foreign troops from Afghanistan. This resolution (ES-6/2, 1980) was carried by 104 votes to 18, with 18 abstentions. Criticism of Soviet intervention was also expressed in other forums, notably the Islamic Council, which condemned Soviet military aggression against the Afghanistan people, called for the withdrawal of Soviet troops, denied recognition of the illegal regime and suspended its membership of the Council.

During 1978–9, as Soviet influence built up in Afghanistan, the Carter Administration had issued warnings about the use of force. There was a sharper message after the US Ambassador to Kabul was killed, apparently by a terrorist group. The Soviet intervention compounded the foreign policy dilemmas faced by President Carter, who was already immersed in the Tehran hostages crisis. Afghanistan raised questions of defining – or redefining – the limits of superpower intervention and influence; this was the first direct introduction of Soviet troops into combat outside the borders of countries occupied by the USSR at the end of the Second World War.

Some response from the United States was obviously necessary: not only was prestige already in question over the Tehran hostage case, but there were potentially serious implications for the western alliance. One interpretation of the Soviet move identified it as part of a global expansionism; the other saw it more narrowly as a defensive and opportunistic response to a number of factors, including the instability produced by the Iranian revolution which had anti-Communist overtones, and a chance to extend Soviet influence to the borders of Pakistan.[12]

In any case, the presence of Soviet forces in Afghanistan had to be treated more seriously than that of Cubans in Angola, Ethiopia and South Yemen. Proximity to the Gulf area, where nearly two-thirds of Japan's and Western Europe's oil imports originate, made it essential to spell out security interests, and in his State of the Union message on 27 January 1980 President Carter stated categorically that an attempt by any outside forces to gain control of the Gulf region would be regarded as an assault on the vital interests of the United States and repelled by any means necessary, including force. But this was a clear signal to deter further expansionism; a response to what had already happened was needed as well.

There was obviously no question of a western military response, nor could non-military measures be sponsored by the UN; they could however be applied on an *ad hoc* basis. In fact the USA promptly imposed a set of measures unilaterally and urged allies to support them *ex post facto*. This they proved very reluctant to do.

President Carter moved swiftly to withdraw the SALT II agreement from the Senate on 7 January and announced a series of measures on 8 January which effectively ended the era of *détente* in US–Soviet economic and cultural relations. These measures involved the closure of the US consulate in Kiev; suspension of cultural and scientific exchanges; withdrawal of Soviet fishing privileges in US waters; a ban on the export of high technology items (to which know-how was added in March) and more rigorous criteria governing exceptions; a ban on the export of 17 million tons of grain for animal consumption (although the 6.8 million tons sold annually under a 1975 agreement between the United States and the Soviet Union was not affected); and a threatened US boycott of the July 1980 Summer Olympics in Moscow if the Soviet Union had not withdrawn its forces from Afghanistan by 20 February.

Administration spokesmen emphasised that although the Soviet intervention was a violation of the UN Charter, particularly Article 2 (4), the US response was within the bounds of law: the measures were unfriendly acts intended to demonstrate disapproval and exact a price for law breaking.

The Soviet leader, Leonid Brezhnev, responded to these announcements by stating that Soviet forces would be withdrawn from Afghanistan when outside interference ceased. Whatever price the Soviet Union may have been forced to pay as a result of the US measures, it did not have to worry about a united Western front. The Canadian Prime Minister was reported as saying later that reactions to Afghanistan were 'absolutely chaotic',[13] and indeed the disarray in the alliance was painfully obvious from the beginning.

At a NATO Council meeting in January there was no agreement on comprehensive sanctions; only the British (Conservative) government supported the boycott of the Olympics, the termination of preferential credit arrangements given to the Soviet Union, and tighter rules for the transfer of technology. France announced it would associate itself with condemnation, but otherwise would pursue an independent policy; President Giscard d'Estaing even met Mr Brezhnev in Warsaw in May. Nor did the EC Foreign Ministers' meeting go beyond cancellation of a food aid programme for Afghanistan, the provision of emergency aid for refugees, and a statement in principle that agricultural exports should not take the place of grain sales embargoed by the United States. Australia, New Zealand and Japan were also restrained in their reaction.

Scepticism over the likely effectiveness of the measures taken by the United States was clearly present in Europe, but there was also a reluctance to take any action which would precipitate a complete abandonment of the *détente* policy of the 1970s and reduce trade and other economic links between East and West Europe which had developed in that period.

By June, Hella Pick was writing in the *Manchester Guardian* that the 'US policy of collective western sanctions against the Kremlin over Afghanistan is in ruins'.[14] Only Britain had withdrawn cheap credit; the EC was allowing the Soviets to buy cheap butter and an animal feed mix which had not previously been purchased and which therefore was not required to be held at 'normal levels'; the West German government set up a new programme of co-operation with the USSR in energy and industrial production at the end of May.

Some brief comments on the grain embargo and the Olympic boycott may be useful in reviewing this episode, and it is also worth looking at the technology transfer question which carried over into the Polish crisis discussed in the next section.

(a) The grain embargo

Soviet dependence on imported grain is unquestioned although it varies according to the size of the domestic harvest. Denial of 17 million tons from the United States could have been quite a serious deprivation, forcing the slaughter of cattle because of a feed shortage, but only if the shortfall could not be made up elsewhere. Hence it was very important for the Carter Administration to have support from other exporting countries particularly Argentina, Australia, Canada and the European Community. A meeting of representatives from these countries was held in Washington, D.C. on 12 January 1980 with the object of obtaining pledges to hold grain sales at existing levels, but there was no solidarity. Australia, Canada and the European Community countries agreed to keep their sales to normal levels but Argentina refused to control sales of grain by destination and the Soviet Union proceeded to buy all it needed from Argentine suppliers. In a study of the embargo, Joseph Hajda has pointed out that in terms of a long-term Soviet–Argentine agreement signed in July 1980 Argentina undertook '... a massive shift of her grain from traditional markets to the Soviet Union, selling ... at premium prices and letting the United States export companies and other suppliers sell in markets that previously were Argentina's'.[15]

Further friction between the allies resulted from Canadian and Australian charges that by concluding a huge wheat deal in China the United States had broken its pledge not to make up its lost grain sales in the traditional markets of others. Within the United States there was bitter opposition to the grain embargo from the farm lobby and in his election campaign Mr Reagan promised to lift it if he became President. This promise was fulfilled on 24 April 1981 (when restrictions on the export of phosphates were also lifted) and talks for a new long-term grain agreement between the United States and the Soviet Union were initiated. There was no question of reimposing the grain embargo during the Polish crisis and this became another source of allied resentment as will be seen below. As a punitive measure it can be described as virtually useless, although it may have had some symbolic effect.[16] In the long run it obviously spurred Soviet efforts to develop self-sufficiency and to treat the United States as a supplier of last resort.

(b) The Olympic boycott

The orchestration of the proposed Olympic boycott led to prolonged and highly publicised arguments between governments and sporting associations at the national and international level, leaving an overall impression of US pressure not on the Soviet

Union but on its Western allies. The continued Soviet military presence in Afghanistan meant that the boycott had to be made official by 24 May, the deadline for acceptance of invitations to participate. The International Olympic Committee, though strongly opposed to the boycott, had to accept the US position. The United States Olympic Committee followed their government's wishes, as did the West German Committee (by a vote of 59 to 40) but the British Olympic Committee rejected their government's advice – and support – and decided to participate. In all, 85 countries accepted invitations, of which about 60 attended (including France, Greece and Iceland); 29 declined and 27 failed to reply. The games suffered from the absence of a number of national teams and overall profit was reduced, but the political impact of the boycott was obviously very limited.

(c) Technology transfer

Controls on trade in strategic goods with communist countries date from the early days of the Cold War. The Co-ordinating Committee (COCOM), consisting of all NATO members except Iceland, and with the addition of Japan, has monitored this trade since 1949, although its activities were originally kept secret and are still handled on a confidential basis.[17] COCOM maintains three international lists covering atomic energy items (including reactors), munitions and military equipment, and industrial items. These lists have been considerably reduced since the 1960s, and West European governments are keen to keep them short, because of their wish to facilitate and develop East–West trade. Each COCOM member also maintains a national list (or lists) and control is exercised at the national level. Exceptions to items embargoed on the COCOM lists can be authorised by consensus.

There have been persistent divisions of opinion between the United States and its allies on the classification of dual-purpose items, with the former favouring a wide and the latter a narrow definition, and also on the definition of strategic technology. As David Baldwin has pointed out, an item is strategic in the context of a specific goal or use; in itself the adjective is meaningless.[18] How can one separate technology for military purposes from that which has industrial uses? And if technology allows resources to be utilised productively, such as technology for oil-drilling equipment, is this a means of strengthening military capability?

President Carter added oil and gas extraction technology to the United States Control List in 1978 – before the Soviet intervention in Afghanistan. The USSR needed western expertise and equipment to develop reserves of oil and natural gas in Siberia; development which from one perspective could be seen as advantageous to the world in that it reduces overall competition for other energy resources, such as Middle East oil. But in a general programme of economic warfare which seeks to retard Soviet economic development, denial of technology can make some sense. Moreover, the US became extremely concerned about the growing dependence of West Europe, and particularly West Germany, on Soviet natural gas as a result of the pipeline project from Siberia which was financed by low interest loans from the west and built with western technology.

The high point of controversy over the pipeline came during the Polish crisis; here it is sufficient to note that the effect of the technology transfer ban, like the effect of the grain embargo and the Olympic boycott, was obviously very limited and largely offset by a shift to Western European suppliers. There was no advance consultation through COCOM before the US ban was imposed.

POLAND

Unrest and guerrilla warfare have continued in Afghanistan but in 1980–1 the focus of world attention shifted to Poland where the struggle between the independent Trade Union Solidarity and the Communist regime brought the danger not only of a collapse of order inside Poland, but also of Soviet military intervention. This was obviously a crisis for NATO and discussions took place within the alliance on contingency policy. The Soviet Union was warned that military intervention would have incalculable consequences, and it was clear that economic sanctions would be imposed even if a NATO military response was out of the question.

In the event, on 13 December 1981, the Polish military, under General Jaruzelski, took control of the government, declared martial law, suspended Solidarity and detained its leaders.

Soviet military intervention would no doubt have been justified by the Kremlin in terms of the Brezhnev Doctrine but if it had taken place, international norm violation would have been easier to assert. Internal repression in Poland, under martial law, with the curtailment of civil liberties, was not a breach of international law and while the situation could be deplored, particularly in the light of Polish pledges under the Helsinki Final Act, there was no obvious legal basis for unilateral or group sanctions by western countries. The Soviet Union could have blocked Security Council action in any case, but there could be no move in the Assembly as for instance over Afghanistan. Nevertheless, the Reagan Administration responded promptly with measures against Poland and against the USSR which it charged with heavy and direct responsibility for martial law. As stated by a senior official to a Congressional committee the steps taken 'demonstrated that the Soviet Union cannot enjoy a normal business relationship with this country after international behaviour which we find totally repugnant'.[19]

Although the grain embargo was not revived, negotiations for a new long-term grain agreement were temporarily shelved. In addition, Aeroflot landing rights in the United States and negotiations for a new agreement on Soviet maritime rights were suspended. The ban on exports of high technology to the USSR, including equipment for the gas pipeline, was tightened. Scientific exchange agreements were not renewed and the Soviet Purchasing Commission was closed. Poland lost landing rights in the US, fishing privileges in US waters and food aid. A freeze was imposed on new official credits and on Export–Import Bank credit insurance. Debt rescheduling negotiations were suspended, as was Poland's most-favoured nation (mfn) status, and its membership in the International Monetary Fund was opposed. Tighter COCOM restrictions were proposed.

Once again the allies were pressed to join the United States in collective measures and once again they proved unwilling. Britain, Canada and Japan imposed some limited diplomatic and economic measures early in 1982, but generally the European view was that economic penalties should not be applied to the USSR unless and until it intervened directly in Poland. Members of the European Community agreed to reduce imports on a very limited range of Soviet luxury goods (caviare, watches, furs) covering about two per cent of all Soviet trade with the EC but generally would not go beyond agreement not to undermine US measures; the preservation of some elements of dialogue and *détente* were felt to take priority while on the specific question of the pipeline the Europeans wished to protect the investment and employment advantages it offered.

The row with the allies took a further turn for the worse in June 1982 when the Reagan Administration banned the export to the Soviet Union by American and foreign firms of oil and gas-related equipment, components and technology except with the permission of the US government.[20] This caused consternation: Canada protested the infringement of its sovereignty[21] while West European governments ordered firms within their jurisdiction to defy the ban and continue to fulfil existing contracts.[22] In response, the United States blacklisted these firms from receiving oil and gas equipment, technology and services from US sources.

The allies thus disagreed with the US on two counts: first, they challenged the justification for 'sanctions'. Retaliation for martial law in Poland, the desire to hurt the Soviet economy and the dangers of undue dependence on Soviet natural gas were not accepted as legitimating penalties. In a leading British newspaper, these explanations of US measures were described as 'a confusing rag-bag of generalisations'.[23] Secondly, they challenged the measures themselves. The sweeping US regulations of June 1982 raised again the vexed question of extraterritoriality which has been a recurring irritant in intra-alliance relations. US anti-trust and securities legislation which has extra-territorial reach, as well as attempts to enforce restrictions on trade with China in the 1950s and Cuba in the 1960s, produced a number of serious disputes, while the freeze of Iranian assets in foreign branches and subsidiaries of US banks in 1980 was regarded as an unjustified extension of US jurisdiction into the sovereignty of European countries.[24] This impingement of measures taken by one government on the jurisdiction of others is one of the serious difficulties raised by 'voluntary' sanctions, in other words, measures not agreed upon within a framework of international authority.

In the summer and early autumn of 1982 the furore over the pipeline tended to overshadow questions of the behaviour of the

Polish and Soviet governments, deepening the image of the Western alliance in disarray. Finally on 13 November 1982, the US withdrew its penalties on European firms and a study of East–West trade was put in hand in NATO. The validity of sanctions against Poland was eventually questioned even by Lech Walesa as making the lot of the Polish people worse; in addition, throughout the crisis there was concern that driving Poland into deeper economic dependence on the Soviet Union or default on her external debt to the west would be counter-productive. Martial law was suspended on 31 December 1982 and a general amnesty for political prisoners was proclaimed in July 1984. President Reagan then officially removed the ban on scientific exchanges and on Polish airline flights to the United States, but the freeze on new credits and cancellation of Poland's most favoured nation status with the US remain in effect at the time of writing. Debt rescheduling discussions resumed as early as November 1982 and in December 1984 the US withdrew its opposition to Polish membership of the International Monetary Fund which opened the prospect of IMF loans in 1986.

The Polish government claimed that the US sanctions had cost $10 million, but it is doubtful if much new credit would have been extended while Poland presented such a poor credit-risk. In fact a *de facto* moratorium on debt repayment by the Polish government since early 1982 helped Poland's foreign exchange problem.

As far as the pipeline is concerned, Reagan Administration spokesmen do not claim that the embargo on parts achieved more than a two-year delay in completion.[25]

The problems of mixed goals and mixed signals are only too obvious from a study of the Afghanistan and Polish crises and they are discussed in detail in the next chapter. The last short case study to be dealt with here is the 1982 Falklands conflict.

THE FALKLANDS CRISIS

The Falklands crisis was of a different character from the other cases discussed in this chapter in that it was initiated and ended by force, but as it provided the occasion for a Security Council determination under Chapter VII of the Charter and for a limited use of economic sanctions by Western governments it is relevant to our concerns.

An Argentinian force seized the Falkland Islands on 2 April 1982. Previous negotiations over sovereignty between Argentina, who declares them to be part of Argentina as Las Malvinas, and Britain, who has been the colonial power since 1833, had not produced an acceptable solution.[26] Regardless of the validity of competing claims, Argentina's action was clearly a violation of Article 2 (4) of the UN Charter.

Realising that an invasion was imminent, Britain went to the Security Council and at an emergency meeting on 3 April Resolution 502 was carried by 10 votes to 1 (Panama) with Poland, Spain and the USSR abstaining.[27] The resolution using Article 39 terminology determined that a breach of the peace existed in the Falklands area, demanded an immediate end to hostilities and the withdrawal of Argentine forces and called for renewed diplomatic negotiations. The British government did not press for sanctions when Argentina failed to comply with this resolution. It was apparently satisfied that Argentina stood condemned by the UN; a Soviet veto might have undermined Britain's case. Meanwhile, acting in self-defence, Britain had dispatched a naval task force to the South Atlantic and on 7 April proclaimed a 200 mile exclusion zone around the Falkland Islands. Argentine assets in Britain, valued at approximately £1000 million were frozen, and an embargo placed on financial transactions and on imports from Argentina. All import licences were revoked; only goods in transit were exempt.

During the rest of April and early May there were unsuccessful efforts to mediate the dispute by US Secretary of State Haig and the UN Secretary-General Perez de Cuellar. Action supportive of the British position was also forthcoming from friends and allies: for instance Canada, Belgium, France, Italy, West Germany and the Netherlands all banned arms sales to Argentina on 7 April. France had been a major supplier of tanks, planes, anti-aircraft missiles, parts and ammunition while West Germany had an $850 million contract for the supply of frigates and corvettes. Britain also urged her European Community partners to adopt collective trade and financial measures against Argentina, banning imports and export credits. Argentine exports to the EC were worth approximately £1013 million in 1980; while its heavy international debt made denial of access to new credit a serious deprivation.

The Ten duly acceded to Britain's request on 16 April, collectively imposing a one-month embargo on arms sales to and imports from Argentina (except all imports which were already licensed, under existing contract or in transit). These Community embargoes were renewed for one week on 16 May, and for an indefinite period on 24 May. Ireland and Italy dissociated themselves from these extensions, but promised not to allow their countries to be used to circumvent the embargoes. In retaliation for what it termed a grave and hostile act, Argentina banned imports of essential products from the Community.

The United States also abandoned its even-handed position at the end of April, signalling its disapproval of Argentina's aggression and support for Britain in the dispute. The Reagan Administration suspended all arms sales to Argentina as well as credit guarantees by the Export–Import Bank and the Commodity Credit Corporation. Most US arms sales had been banned since 1978 because of the Argentine junta's poor human rights record.

Argentina appealed to the OAS for help but no more than rhetorical support was forthcoming with Chile, Colombia and Trinidad and Tobago joining the United States in opposition to the Argentine position. At a special meeting of OAS Foreign Ministers in Washington, DC from 26–8 April, a resolution was passed by 17 to none (with 4 abstentions and 8 non-participants) recognising Argentina's sovereignty over Las Malvinas and calling on Britain to cease hostilities. There was no mention of the Rio Treaty. The resolution also deplored the 'coercive measures' adopted by the EC and other governments; these were described as prejudicial to Argentina and a serious precedent, not covered by Resolution 502 and incompatible with the UN Charter and GATT. It was difficult for the OAS to defend Argentina's conduct in the face of a Security Council condemnation; nor was seizure of contested territory by force a welcome precedent for some of its members.

Meanwhile Prime Minister Thatcher announced on 20 May that diplomacy had failed and withdrew all offers from the negotiating table. In the following weeks the Falkland Islands were recaptured by British forces. The Argentine military commander surrendered on 14 June.

From 27–9 May there had been another (emergency) meeting of the OAS Foreign Ministers, held in camera. Argentina wanted sanctions but the resolution adopted (by 17 : 0 with Chile, Colombia, Trinidad and Tobago and the United States abstaining as before) merely condemned the British attack and called on the US to support 'regional solidarity' by lifting its coercive measures against Argentina and discontinuing aid to Britain. The resolution did not refer to Security Council Resolution 502, and was inconsistent with it.[28]

Once the fighting was over, there was a progressive trend to normalisation of Argentina's external economic relations. General Galtieri resigned as President and Commander-in-chief on 17 June and by 1 July a largely civilian government under General Bignone had taken office. The British blockade was lifted on 22 July but EC measures had been removed on 21 June and Canada, Norway and Japan had also resumed normal trade. The United States removed economic restrictions in July and allowed trade in spare parts for military equipment to resume in August but Administration certification for the resumption of arms sales and military assistance was not given until December 1983, by which time democratic rule under President Alfonsin had been restored. France resumed arms sales to Argentina in early August 1982 and West Germany and Italy soon followed suit.

Britain and Argentina reciprocally lifted financial restrictions on 14 September 1982 to pave the way for help for Argentina's distressed economy from the International Monetary Fund, but the continuing dispute over sovereignty delayed normalisation of trade. On 8 July 1985 Britain unilaterally lifted the ban on imports from Argentina hoping to recover sales of machinery and industrial products worth £150 million in 1982. The British government reiterated its position that 'the question of sovereignty over the islands is not for discussion'.[29] The Argentine government did not immediately reciprocate but reiterated its call for talks on sovereignty.

The interest of the Falklands case for this study is not primarily the economic impact of the sanctions which were only in effect as far as the EC and all other countries (except Britain) were concerned for a period of between two and three months. The financial and trade restrictions were certainly unwelcome, given the already precarious state of the Argentine economy and its massive indebtedness and in a longer war the arms embargo could have been a significant factor. Peter Calvert notes that military supplies for Argentina were actually flown from Stansted Airport in Britain up to two days before the invasion 'and most commercial cargoes were in transit long after that'.[30] It is worth noting, too, that Argentina's retaliation was limited; goods needed 'in the national interest' were not embargoed.[31] But the significance of the episode lies in the demonstration of collective support for Britain's position, particularly in the unprecedented solidarity of the European Community which made an important political statement in support of the UN Charter's ban on the use of force, backing up Security Council Resolution 502. This kind of solidarity would have been welcomed by the United States in earlier crises over Iran, Afghanistan and Poland, but it had not been forthcoming. Of course the seizure of the Falklands was 'traditional' wrong-doing of the kind envisaged by the League Covenant and the UN Charter as calling for international sanctions, and the measures imposed by Britain's friends and allies went beyond 'multiple unilateralism' in that they could draw authority from Resolution 502. Action by the OAS under Chapter viii of the Charter was also blocked by this resolution.

It has been argued that the undeniable demonstration effect created by the EC sanctions would have been greatly strengthened had the United States not tried to play a mediatory role, but come down firmly on Britain's side from the beginning; in these circumstances the Argentine Junta might have been more amenable to a withdrawal of forces with a view to diplomatic bargaining being resumed.[32] This can only be conjecture. What is certain is that the collective response had political and psychic impact, enhanced on the one hand by UN Security Council Resolution 502 which identified wrong-doing, and on the other by the extent and cohesion of the sanctioning group.

7 Problems for States Applying Sanctions

This chapter focuses on the major issues and problems faced by governments who resort to collective sanctions. Group decisions are more difficult to take and to implement than individual decisions; where interests diverge, compromise is needed to achieve consensus. Concerted international action requires co-operation in policy making and policy implementation by states of different size and strength who may have different values and competing ideologies. Each will be jealous of its own sovereignty and prestige and intent on pursuing national goals. Moreover governments are responsible to their domestic constituencies and cannot be seen as neglectful of domestic interests.

The process of decision making about sanctions must begin with consideration of the grounds for threatening or imposing them and of the purposes they are designed to serve. These questions of motive and intention are closely linked to the choice of particular measures. Expected impact is obviously important, but so is expected cost. 'Expensive' sanctions, such as export embargoes, will not commend themselves to governments pursuing domestic goals of increased employment and economic growth; nor will governments wish to alienate politically influential domestic groups whose interests will be adversely affected by sanctions. On the other hand, failure to take action may weaken a government's position domestically and elicit disapproval and even retaliation from other governments. In other words both policy costs and political costs will have to be considered.[1] Further problems arise in respect of co-ordinating the collective effort to maximise its impact. Initial agreement is difficult to achieve at the best of times, and continuing solidarity is very hard to maintain. If governments are out of step with each other to begin with, it will be almost impossible to get into step later. Finally, even if consensus is reached and sustained, a government can face obstacles and difficulties with sanctions implementation within its own political system, particularly if it has to rely on the voluntary co-operation of the private sector.

The case studies outlined in preceding chapters provide excellent illustration of all these problems. In wartime, when defeating the enemy is the overriding concern, some of them are less acute, or even non-existent. Sacrifice is accepted as part of a national war effort and anything which contributes to the enemy's war potential is an obvious target for interdiction. Economic, financial, cultural and communications links will automatically be severed while the major policy instrument will be force. But even in wartime, where defeat of the enemy provides a single common goal, serious disagreement can arise, as between the Soviet Union and the Western Powers between 1941 and 1945. In a cold war situation, policy co-ordination among allies is obviously more complex. The precise goal of military defeat is absent and there may be varying perceptions of threat. Growing and highly visible strains in the Western alliance over the past decade reflect not only differences over tactical moves between the United States on the one hand and Western Europe (and usually) Canada and Japan on the other, but a serious divergence of views over the nature of East–West relations and the strategies which are appropriate to their conduct. In other words, it is not just a question of whether, or how, the USSR and Poland should be punished for the imposition of martial law in the latter country, but of different perceptions of Soviet intentions and of the nature of the communist threat.[2] Nevertheless, there are still some shared parameters. There is a common concern about Soviet expansionism and basic agreement on defensive/protective policies. No western government believes that arms or military materiel should be exported to the USSR.

The bases for collective retaliation become more shaky when relations between the miscreant and the sanctioning states are not bad, or are even quite good. As we have seen in earlier chapters, founders of the League and the United Nations tried to inject some order and predictability into the sanctioning process, first by defining wrong-doing (in the Covenant) and by giving the Security Council authority to define it (in the Charter); secondly by imposing obligations on members to apply sanctions (under the Covenant) and to obey the Security Council (under the Charter). In practice, order and predictability have failed to materialise. League members were reluctant to fulfil their obligations while in the UN enforcement was stillborn.

Members of the Security Council rarely agree on offences or on culpability and are not prepared to bear the risks and costs of imposing penalties. Within organisations or blocs at the regional level, there is perhaps a greater chance of shared values and perceptions, but also of standards and responses being coerced by a disproportionately powerful member of the group.

Outside the framework of organisations and blocs, the scope for disagreement is boundless. What motivates support for a collective response by states whose interests are not directly challenged? Respect for community values? The need or wish to assist a friend or ally? In this open situation, which now appears to be more typical than cases of structured, organisational sanctions, all kinds of policy priorities jostle for precedence. There are no fixed or prior commitments and intragroup bargaining can produce intra-group threatened or actual punishments.

MOTIVES AND PURPOSES

The logical point of departure for this discussion is the purpose of sanctions. Within the UN (as earlier within the League of Nations) the formal role of sanctions is to defend community values by threatening or actually imposing penalties on those who break the rules. Acts of aggression, breaches of the peace and threats to the peace, identified in those terms by the Security Council, should be the occasion for a group response. In such circumstances, it might be supposed the objective of the sanctioning group would be to end the conflict, or remove the threat. These and other target-related goals are usually relevant and, irrespective of the presence or absence of an authoritative framework for sanctions, those imposing them are likely to stress the unacceptable behaviour of the target and their own role in defending community interests at some cost to themselves (for instance, 'aggression must not pay'). But a much more complex mix of objectives needs to be unravelled. As James Barber was one of the first to point out,[3] motives for imposing sanctions may be explained by domestic pressures, and third parties may also be relevant to policy considerations. Moreover, governments do not necessarily disclose the full range of considerations which lead them to take sanctioning decisions, and one needs to look beyond the ostensible goals set out in public statements.

For purposes of analysis, targets, domestic audiences and third parties will be considered separately, although in practice governments may hope to achieve results in two or more areas.

(a) **Target-related goals**

A sharp change in policy by the target may indeed be the principal objective and preferred outcome of sanctions; for example, an Italian withdrawal from Ethiopia or an Argentine withdrawal from the Falkland Islands. In the League system, unlawful war was the only basis for sanctions, but a wider range of objectives is possible under the terms of Chapter VII of the Charter, encompassing domestic as well as foreign policies of targets. The Security Council can order preventive as well as remedial action; given great power unanimity and adequate support from other members, it can designate any situation a threat to the peace. In some cases, the purpose of sanctions may not be to restore the status quo but to alter it. South Africa is a case in point.

This represents a considerable development of the whole concept of the use of international sanctions, permitting the Security Council to define wrong-doing in the context of new norms of decolonisation, non-discrimination and human rights. As established in Chapter 2, the Security Council's authority to condemn internal situations in member countries is superior to that of regional bodies or groupings which take such stands, as well as to that of individual members, but it is hard to force radical internal political change by non-military sanctions. Not only will pressure for such change be regarded as improper intervention by the target, but among those considering or applying sanctions there will be scope for widely divergent views as to the extent and degree of reform needed. Ending a foreign war may restore peace and stability; engendering internal change may actually spawn instability and turmoil. If peaceful, legitimised change is sought, there must also be acceptance of the new system by the inhabitants of the country concerned.

Both the Rhodesian and South African cases illustrate these difficulties. Mandatory UN sanctions were imposed on Rhodesia to meet a designated threat to the peace, but the superficial consensus over the need to remove this threat concealed a complex of attitudes and aspirations. Britain's primary aim was

the restoration of constitutional government and the introduction of eventual majority rule for Africans in the territory;
under these conditions, the British government would have been
prepared to initiate negotiations for granting formal independence. But as Britain could not or would not impose a
settlement, recourse to the UN was a means of sharing responsibility and of satisfying Commonwealth demands for action.
Once the UN became directly involved, the objectives of African
states in supporting sanctions and calling for sterner measures
were also reflected in sanctions policy. These objectives were
more far-reaching, encompassing the elimination of white minority rule in Rhodesia.

In South Africa western industrialised nations wish to see the
end of apartheid and the evolution of democracy but they do
not (yet) support mandatory sanctions as a means of forcing
change. Their concern is as much for stability as for reform.
Again African countries have a different perspective, seeing
sanctions as a necessary kind of international pressure. Even
among Third World states, however, there could be disagreement on the preferred form of ultimate political system for
South Africa, while within South Africa itself there is obviously
a wide spectrum of possible positions.

The record of international sanctions of a non-military kind,
even when applied within an organisational framework, suggests
that on their own they will not succeed in drastically altering
the foreign or domestic policy of the target. The pressure exerted
has proved inadequate and the means and will to resist it have
been too strong. Governments are aware of this and frequently
use it as a justification for *not* imposing sanctions; if they do
decide to impose them they will not necessarily rule out coercive
impact but usually protect themselves from later accusations of
failure by asserting that punishment, not target compliance, is
the object of the exercise. In other words, sanctions are presented
as measures which make life more difficult for the target by
attaching a cost, or price to its conduct; a kind of fine for
international misbehaviour. For instance, the US explanation
for sanctions against Cuba included demonstrating to the Cuban
people that the Castro regime did not serve their interests, while
in 1980 US Secretary of State Muskie stated that measures
taken against the Soviet Union after Afghanistan were intended
'to demonstrate that aggression bears a price ...'.[4]

Another role for sanctions is to demonstrate commitment to a position. Economic or political measures signal disapproval in a non-lethal manner which is more telling than verbal censure, a point strongly emphasised by those advocating sanctions against South Africa. The European Community's economic sanctions against Argentina in the Falklands crisis signalled strong disapproval of Argentina's resort to force and showed willingness to incur some inconvenience to make the point. Of course in this case the economic measures were secondary, as Britain recovered the islands by military means. Short-term gestures of protest can also have a demonstrative effect: the cancellation of Aeroflot flights to Canada and certain West European countries for a limited period after the shooting down of Korean Air Lines Flight 007 by a Soviet fighter plane in September 1983 made disapproval clear and pointed.

David Baldwin has pointed out that sanctions can be intended to signal more than disapproval by confirming the willingness of sanctioning state(s) to adopt stronger measures if the target's policies continue to give offence.[5] As a form of compellence, the Commonwealth Heads of Governments' decision in October 1985 to impose mild economic sanctions on South Africa, with the promise of more severe measures in six months' time if no progress had been made in dismantling apartheid, sought to combine punishment and threat, although Mrs Thatcher's clearly stated aversion to stronger sanctions obviously reduced the credibility of the threat.

In the case of the US grain embargo against the Soviet Union imposed after the intervention in Afghanistan, Baldwin argues persuasively that its primary purpose was to warn the Soviet government that further action would be taken to counter any attempt to extend Soviet influence in west Asia; the fact that the embargo imposed higher costs on the United States than on the USSR is seen as having enhanced 'the credibility of the message' which was therefore one of deterrence.[6]

In general, one accepts that willingness to incur material sacrifice for the sake of upholding moral or legal principles has a significant demonstration effect, but there are some risks attached to the kind of complex signalling attributed to the Carter Administration over Afghanistan, in that the message or messages may be misunderstood by the target. It is also worth noting that mild sanctions may be imposed not as a warning of severer measures to come, but for pre-emptive reasons. In other words, the sanctions represent 'something' in the way of a response, rather than 'nothing', but are deliberately chosen to minimise cost and dislocation while symbolising a willingness to act. The implications of such a policy are discussed further below.

Before leaving the discussion of target-related goals, it is worth noting that pursuing the imposition of sanctions as an objective can itself serve the political objective of consciousness-raising. Repeated efforts at the UN to convert Western governments to a pro-sanctions position regarding South Africa and formerly Rhodesia are part of the calculated political strategy adopted by Third World countries to isolate white minority regimes and keep their faults on all international agenda and in the spotlight of public opinion.[7] A campaign for sanctions publicises the cause. Media attention is focused on the mis-behaviour of the target regime and its legitimacy is eroded, while proposals for sanctions in international forums force governments to define their positions publicly, and builds pressure for condemning rather than condoning the situation. Ultimately opposition to sanctions can become synonymous with support for apartheid.

(b) The domestic audience

Some public statement explaining the reason for sanctions and the purposes they are ostensibly intended to serve is to be expected from governments applying them. As noted above, such statements are unlikely to tell the full story. It is hardly to be expected that governments will publicise their motives and intentions if doing so would cause them embarrassment.

Sanctions can be a means of satisfying influential sections of the population who demand retaliation for the conduct of foreign states, and they may also serve other domestic purposes. Moves by Republicans in the US Congress to act against South Africa may be partly explained by reluctance to leave the moral high ground to the Democrats for whom human rights in South Africa have become a rallying point, supported vigorously by Black Americans. Where there appears to be a direct threat to national interests, sanctions can reflect governmental purposiveness and strength, which can improve popularity and electoral prospects. Prestige and national pride cannot be discounted as significant political factors, and repeated failure to respond to perceived external 'challenges' may suggest a lack of will or resolve on the part of national leaders. This will be particularly unwelcome for leaders of powerful states. In the context of intense antagonism and rivalry such as exists between the United States and the Soviet Union, the drive for retaliation is particularly strong, so that tit-for-tatism becomes endemic.

(c) Third parties

Sanctions may also carry messages to third parties and part of the motive for retaliation may be exemplary – demonstrating to third states the likely costs of misbehaviour. Sanctions may also be imposed, willingly or under pressure, to show solidarity with friends and allies. As a motivating factor, the defence of an international norm may be less important than pressure from an alliance partner. The reluctance of West European governments to take measures against Iran and the Soviet Union in the wake of the crises in Tehran and Afghanistan was patent, and a powerful factor in inducing them to take any action at all was clearly the expressed wish of the United States Administration that they should do so.[8] Even more telling in this connection was the dispute between the Europeans and the United States over the export of equipment and technology for the Siberian gas pipeline which the United States sought to ban in the wake of the Polish crisis. The penalties imposed by the United States on European firms who defied the ban and continued to make deliveries to the USSR under existing contracts (as required by their own governments) were widely referred to in the media as 'sanctions', which confused the issue as to who was being punished for what. The Reagan Administration was subjected to strong criticism from the European Community on this issue and there were also domestic pressures for the withdrawal of the offending regulations. They were lifted on 13 November 1982 with the face-saving announcement that there was now 'substantial agreement' among the Allies for increased control of East–West trade.[9] The point to be made in the context of a discussion of objectives is that in this particular case, the wish of West Europeans to please their ally, the United States, took second place to their wish to continue economic linkages with the East which had been forged in the period of *détente*, particularly linkages which diversified sources of energy.

South Africa, like Rhodesia in the 1960s and 1970s, may provoke Commonwealth pressure on Britain to adopt a wide range of sanctions; failure to respond could damage the viability of the association.

(d) General goals of foreign policy

It is also possible that the actions or policies of one state will present an opportunity for others to satisfy goals of their own by resorting to 'retaliatory' measures. Measures presented as sanctions can be a useful tactic in an on-going policy strategy rather than a discrete response to a discrete and unacceptable act. Action against Argentina by Britain, the United States, the European Community and Commonwealth countries was specifically linked to the seizure of the Falklands, in the same way that League of Nations sanctions against Italy were occasioned by Mussolini's invasion of Ethiopia. These sanctions were imposed reluctantly by governments which, other things being equal, would have preferred to remain on friendly terms with the target. In contrast, action against the USSR for its intervention in Afghanistan, and even more noticeably for its connection with the Polish crisis, can be viewed as further stages in the Cold War which has characterised superpower relationships since the end of the Second World War. By the same token the measures which the US imposed and tried hard to persuade its allies to support were an intensification of the controls on East–West economic relations which have existed since 1947, but which were progressively relaxed in the years of *détente*. Co-ordinated by COCOM these controls have sought to prevent, or at least to hinder the growth of the Soviet economy and to limit Soviet military capability; as such they are weapons of (cold) economic warfare.[10] One can say that by denying the Soviet Union high technology items the West, under US leadership, is in a sense penalising Soviet ideological and strategic goals, but this is linked to the wider goals of containment and undermining the Soviet economy and is of a different order from penalties for breaches of international law or morality.

It goes without saying that governments do not pursue one foreign policy goal at a time nor are all goals mutually reinforcing. The simultaneous or overlapping pursuit of conflicting objectives is quite common and undermines the impact of sanctions. A clear example from our case studies is the dual policy by which Britain and France sought to support the League of Nations and conciliate Mussolini at the same time. The series of confused explanations given by the Reagan Administration for sanctions against Poland and the USSR was recorded in the previous chapter and coherent policy is unlikely to be the product of numerous centres of decision making. The multiplicity of departments and agencies handling US foreign policy is generally not conducive to the clear definition and pursuit of foreign policy goals, and other governments have similar problems.

All cases of sanctions will probably exhibit a mixture of goals and objectives related not only to ostensible targets but also to domestic constituencies and third parties. Pressures from internal sources to impose (or not impose) sanctions will have to be reconciled with pressures from external sources and with the government's own positions and policies. The trend to *ad hoc* retaliation, outside any organisational framework makes it likely that the specific domestic and foreign policy objectives of individual states, particularly powerful states, will play a strong or even decisive role, while claims to be acting in defence of principle and international law will not necessarily be convincing. To proceed beyond the general survey of motives attempted in this section would require very detailed investigation of individual case studies.

SELECTION OF MEASURES

Further problems are likely to arise when a group of governments seeks agreement on appropriate collective measures. Inside international organisations a prescribed range of penalties to fit designated offences scarcely exists: the total boycott provisions of Article 16 of the Covenant were rapidly abandoned by League members in favour of selective and graduated penalties, while in the United Nations Charter it is left to the Security Council to impose any combination of non-military measures thought appropriate. Similar latitude exists in regional charters.

The most specific penalties in the UN Charter relate to suspension and expulsion; functional agencies can withdraw services and privileges associated with membership. Outside the
framework of international organisations, the field is open. Non-
military measures include political, diplomatic and cultural penalties and the full range of economic penalties from embargoes
on financial and commercial dealings to the restriction or severance of transportation and communication. A detailed list was
given at the end of Chapter 1.

Crucial factors influencing the choice of particular measures
adopted singly or in combination would be the objectives sought,
the vulnerability and sensitivity of the delinquent state, and the
minimisation of cost and damage to the sanctioning group. The
complexity of stated and unstated objectives has already been
explored. In particular, the salience of target-related goals needs
to be carefully assessed. If the main reason for imposing sanctions is pre-emptive – doing something rather than nothing, to
appease internal or external pressure groups – then 'something'
is likely to be 'as little as possible'.

Judgements about the vulnerability of the target to political
and economic pressure will be extremely hard to make. Even
the economic effects of different kinds of economic sanction
cannot be precisely estimated in advance. There are too many
uncertainties, not only in respect of the target's reaction, but
also the reactions of other states. For instance, in his study of
sanctions against Rhodesia, Strack cites a report prepared for
the UN Secretary-General by a New York consulting firm which
correctly forecast the 'potency of an oil embargo to directly and
quickly affect the [Rhodesian] population' but incorrectly judged
first that South Africa would not bail Rhodesia out because of
its own dependence on imported oil and fear of incurring sanctions itself, and second that indirect methods of supplying Rhodesia would not be efficacious.[11]

The range of defensive measures available to target states is
discussed in the next chapter, but it is obvious that no state
will be completely devoid of adaptive and evasive strategies.
Dependence on foreign trade, whether as a source of foreign
exchange earned by exports or as a source of vital imports, or
both, and dependence on foreign investment, or foreign aid,
obviously suggest utilisation of commercial or financial embargoes by sanctioning states but it is very hard to predict how

strongly and soon such measures will impact on the target economy. The Rhodesian case showed that if target governments can 'weather' the initial 'storm' of economic sanctions, those imposing them face a long haul. This not only gives the target opportunities to overcome or circumvent the sanctions but also puts a strain on the solidarity of the sanctioning group: second thoughts, backsliding, and pressure for an end to sanctions from groups adversely affected can all be confidently predicted. As time passes, reluctance to forego profitable trade and investment is likely to increase rather than decrease, especially in hard economic times.

It will also be virtually impossible to calculate with any degree of precision the probable reaction of individuals or groups in a target state to externally-induced falls in income levels. There may be an unforeseen willingness to accept a measure of sacrifice, and falls in real income produced by sanctions may not be sufficient either to persuade the government of the target, under pressure from its citizens, to change its policy, or to bring an alternative government into power.[12] The situation becomes even less calculable if the desired change in policy would itself bring, or would be expected to bring, lower incomes or a fall in the standard of living of politically-influential sectors of the population, an aspect of sanctions which was particularly relevant to the Rhodesian case, and would also apply to South Africa.

On the other hand, if vulnerability to vital imports, particularly energy supplies, can be effectively exploited, it is possible that target governments might become more amenable. Mussolini evidently feared an oil sanction so much that he deterred it by threatening it would mean war; if Rhodesia had not continued to receive oil through Mozambique and South Africa, the Smith regime might have fulfilled Harold Wilson's prediction and collapsed in a matter of weeks. Certainly the Arab oil embargoes in 1973–4 showed that countries like Japan, Israel and South Africa would be in serious difficulties if oil could no longer be imported. But this would require a degree of unanimity among all suppliers which has not yet been attained; the problem of 'gaps' in the sanctions front is discussed in the final section of this chapter.

It has been the failure of international sanctions to bring conclusive results which has undermined confidence in their efficacy. More modest objectives are more easily realised; for instance, to give the target an economic 'slap on the wrist', to add to its economic difficulties on a continuing basis, or simply to draw attention to its wrong-doing through international publicity.

COSTS

International organisations provide a basis for co-ordinating decisions about sanctions: whether to impose them and what measures to choose. A decision by the Security Council obligates members to act. Bodies such as the OAS and the EC acting against members (or non-members) also have a formal structure which facilitates group decision making. The EC is obviously in a good position to organise decisions on trade sanctions. Action taken outside organisational frameworks – 'multiple unilateralism' – is likely to involve disputed and badly co-ordinated measures which may also arouse resentment because the burdens are perceived to be inequitable. In practice the element of cost can be expected to play a very significant role in all sanctioning decisions, even in the unlikely event of a mandatory order from the Security Council. Debates about the merits of certain measures allow individual governments to plead damaging impact on their own domestic economies. Exemptions weaken the whole effort: as an authority on the League's only sanctions experiment commented 'the acid of exemptions will eat the very heart out of the sanctions system'.[13] Outside the UN framework, equity of sacrifice becomes a very controversial issue. Both NATO and the EC have experienced discord over burden sharing associated with agreed policies; if the policies themselves are challenged the scope for friction and disagreement is considerably wider. The European refusal to embargo equipment for the Siberian gas pipeline was a case in point, particularly in the light of the American refusal to reinstate a grain embargo. In European eyes, the United States was making no sacrifice at all; in 1980 the dollar value of EC trade with Eastern Europe was ten times that of US trade with the same region.

In making cost assessments, perception and judgement will be crucial. Positive and negative aspects of applying sanctions will be assessed along a number of dimensions: political, strategic, economic, psychological. Inevitably there will be problems of aggregation. The multiplicity of possible objectives described earlier in this chapter is a further complication. Cost–benefit equations will differ if the chief purpose of sanctions is to satisfy a domestic pressure group rather than to placate an ally, defend an international norm, or signal commitment to a position.

Presumably one can safely assert that a threat of punitive sanctions is more economical than their actual imposition, but once imposed, their utility in terms of impact on the target, and satisfaction of domestic or other goals will have to be weighed against the loss of advantage they represent in terms of increased hostility and possible counter-measures from the target, and irritation or alienation of allies,[14] as well as in more readily quantifiable areas such as markets or supplies forfeited as a result of export or import embargoes. There may also be a negative reaction from influential sectors of the domestic population; American farmers were outraged by the partial grain embargo imposed by the Carter Administration after the Soviet intervention in Afghanistan. Mr Reagan's campaign promise to lift the embargo was carried out once he was elected President, and it was not reinstated, in spite of his Administration's imposition of other penalties on the Soviet Union.

It should also be noted that assessments of the cost of sanctions may prove to be inaccurate. The target's response is unpredictable and other consequences must be considered. One must question whether the US expected that its allies would prove so reluctant to join in its sanctions against the USSR and Poland and whether the damage to the western alliance was justified in terms of pain inflicted on the targets. The cost of the pipeline embargo had not been thought through on its own merits: in a Note to the US Administration, EC members complained that the ban on the supply of technology for the Siberian pipeline 'applied retroactively and without sufficient consultation ... [was] ... unquestionably and seriously damaging'.[15] It was pointed out that in the short term some companies which had made investments and commitments to the project might not survive at all while others would suffer a loss of business that would lead to unemployment; in the long run, the disruption of contracts 'concluded in good faith' would damage the image of European companies 'as reliable suppliers in the eyes not only of the Soviet Union, but also of ... actual and potential business partners in other countries'.[16]

Summing up this discussion it is probably safe to say that the estimated minimum cost to sanctioning states, consistent with the satisfaction of objectives, is likely to be an overriding factor in the choice of measures and for this reason, milder or even symbolic measures may be preferred. Wider costs to the international economic and financial system are dealt with in the next chapter.

THE SCOPE OF SANCTIONING PROGRAMMES

The universal application of sanctions represents the ideal rather than the attainable situation. It is unrealistic to envisage all countries, whether members of the United Nations or not, co-operating fully in imposing a total boycott on economic relations with a delinquent state. This was the goal of Article 16 of the League Covenant, picturesquely described as a 'revival of medieval excommunication'.[17] Neither the League nor the UN has achieved more than partial application of economic sanctions, while sanctioning at the regional level and *ad hoc* group sanctions are obviously subject to inherent limitations.

Without universality of application or a physical blockade, vulnerability to external economic pressure is drastically lessened. The existence of non-participants in enforcement brings possibilities of important trading relationships being left untouched by sanctions; of alternative markets and sources of supply becoming available; of evasive action being channelled through third states; of loans, credits, and even gifts from friendly powers; and the development of new communications and lines of transport to replace those cut by sanctions. The psychological effect of the sanctions policy will also be weakened.

The League was at a permanent disadvantage because major trading nations, particularly the United States, were not members and could supply the essential needs of any target of sanctions, thereby making the economic weapon more than usually blunt. Moreover Germany and Japan, after leaving the League in the 1930s, were not likely to be co-operative. But the problem of non-members is only one limitation on international enforcement facing members of an international organisation;

the other is the problem of members who do not participate. In the case of Italy several League members continued normal trade leaving a wide gap in the sanctions front. Austria, Albania and Hungary were the chief offenders and their proximity to Italy made their defection a serious matter. A proposal was made to reduce imports from non-participating states to the extent to which they benefited from sanctions, but it was not implemented.

The Charter sought to overcome the problem by providing that UN members must comply with Security Council decisions, but although the UN has achieved virtual universality of membership, failure to observe the obligations imposed by the Charter does not automatically lead to the imposition of any penalty. The logical outcome would be the extension of sanctions to the defaulting member(s), but this would involve further cost and dislocation of trade for the sanctioning group. Moreover, *recommendations* of the Assembly or the Security Council do not *require* compliance.

The measures selected as sanctions against Rhodesia were more comprehensive than those imposed on Italy by the League in 1935, but they were not made total until May 1968. This delay, however, was probably less important than the partial scope of their application. Switzerland, a non-member of the UN, was not sympathetic to the illegal regime but it adopted a neutral stance and permitted limited trade, while two members Portugal (until 1974) and South Africa played a crucial role in helping Rhodesia to survive. After UN sanctions were imposed, the South African government ignored all inquiries from the United Nations about its trade with Rhodesia. It did not recognise the independence of Rhodesia *de jure*; but *de facto* and close relations were maintained with the Rhodesian government. Both Portugal and South Africa probably felt confident that in defying the United Nations they would not bring retribution on their own heads: it was no secret that Britain was not prepared to sponsor punitive measures against them.

The Portuguese situation changed after the fall of Salazar and the independence of Angola and Mozambique, but South Africa continued to give economic assistance to the Rhodesian regime. Moreover, it is clear that UN sanctions, particularly the oil sanction, were being evaded from the very early days. The revelations of the Bingham Report and other documentation described in Chapter 4 show that oil swap arrangements between British and French oil companies made it possible for Rhodesia to obtain oil via South Africa; the Beira blockade by a British naval patrol was a farce at the British taxpayer's expense. In addition to this glaring gap in sanctions implementation, circuitous means of exporting and importing were in use throughout the sanctions era and for several years the US openly imported chrome, nickel and other materials from Rhodesia in violation of its obligations under the UN Charter.

The limitations of programmes of economic denial which – however comprehensive – are applied by regional groupings of states but not backed by force are illustrated by the experience of Cuba in the Western hemisphere. When embargoes were imposed on Cuba by the United States and the OAS, the United States was Cuba's leading trading partner. But Cuba proceeded to draw material and ideological support from the Soviet Union which assumed a dominant role in Cuban economic life and assisted the regime of Fidel Castro to continue its programme of economic and social development. The achievement of Yugoslavia and Albania in reorienting economic relationships under Soviet pressure is further evidence of the importance of third-party support. In all these regional cases, support was forthcoming from another major power or power grouping which enabled the target regime to survive. Without such support the situation could obviously be very much more precarious and if other interventionary tactics are used besides diplomatic and economic penalties, such as support of internal factions opposed to the target government (perhaps even of a guerrilla group), or if a naval blockade effectively isolates the target, or military intervention takes place, the target regime could fall.

Unanimity within international bodies is often elusive, but if a decision is reached to impose sanctions there is some minimum degree of accord. At least there will be a clarification of the offence and some statement of intention regarding the collective response. The situation is much more problematical in cases of non-organisational sanctions which may be very limited in scope and implementation.

As noted in Chapter 6, in discussion of sanctions against Iran, Poland and the USSR, there was overt pressure by the United States on its western allies to join in measures which it had already announced. Synchronisation was lacking from the outset. Where Cold War issues intrude, the United States clearly expects co-operation in its 'sanctions' and is prepared to threaten or even impose penalties if it is not forthcoming. These second order penalties have a long history. The strategic embargoes orchestrated by COCOM have already been mentioned; the sanctions imposed on Cuba by the United States and later the OAS were the occasion of heavy pressure by the United States on Canada, Japan and West European countries to join in. They were not at all enthusiastic, being unwilling to forego trade with Cuba to suit US policy.[18] Not only had their interests in Cuba been treated less harshly than American interests, but Cuba was a good customer for countries actively seeking export contracts and sales. The Johnson Administration's considerable efforts to bring about Cuba's economic isolation did have some early success, although full co-operation was not forthcoming from the allies and considerable friction ensued, but by the end of the 1960s it has been reckoned a failure.[19]

Clearly in a programme of economic pressure against Cuba, the roles of Canada and Britain were far more important than those of OAS members, although the United States no doubt saw OAS backing as enhancing the legitimacy of sanctions. These efforts at leverage were not all one-way, as the case of Spain illustrates. The Spanish government was very much opposed to embargoes on trade with Cuba and the US need for a continuation of military bases in Spain gave some bargaining strength to the smaller power.[20]

Ad hoc sanctions against Iran, Poland, the USSR and Argentina were obviously all of limited scope. Blocked supplies were usually available from alternative sources and the lack-lustre attitude of Western allies to the sanctions against Iran, Poland and the USSR weakened their impact in symbolic and real terms. The US arm-twisting over the Afghanistan and Polish crises could not be based on charges that the allies were failing to carry out legal obligations, only that they were letting down the side. This is an argument based on emotion and may produce a tendency to exaggerate the alleged enormity of the crime, thus exacerbating the crisis.

Ironically, the secondary pressure applied to allies may be felt and resented as keenly as the primary pressure applied to the target, particularly where the latter occurs in an ongoing Cold War situation and is therefore expected and discounted.

Displays of disagreement and resistance to jurisdictional expans-
iveness (extra-territoriality) weaken the image of 'rightness' of a
cause; thus *ad hoc* group retaliation becomes less recognisable
as 'sanctions' and indistinguishable from foreign policy acts of
a self-serving kind.

IMPLEMENTATION

Finally, a group of countries contemplating collective sanctions
face major problems of implementation and control at the
national and international level. During the Second World War,
the allied economic effort was effectively co-ordinated, with
close liaison maintained between British and US government
departments, and mention has already been made of COCOM
which co-ordinates the application of western strategic controls
on trade with the USSR. But the actual implementation of
controls in all cases must be handled by national systems.
No international organisation can apply import and export
embargoes or financial, transportation or diplomatic sanctions
which fall under the jurisdiction of national governments; it can
only act within its own range of powers to enforce penalties in
respect of voting privileges, membership, or access to development finance.

Neither the League nor the UN set up standing machinery
for sanctions supervision. In the Italian case, procedures were
devised on an *ad hoc* basis,[21] involving a general Co-ordinating
Committee of all members with an executive Committee of
Eighteen responsible for proposing measures, collecting government responses and maintaining liaison with non-members.
Three sub-committees dealt with economic measures, financial
measures and mutual support and there were also committees
of legal and military experts. Discussions took place with governments on their intentions and on their legislative competence to
apply sanctions and a system of reporting exports and imports
was instituted through use of a questionnaire. The Committee
of Eighteen also commissioned a special report on the feasibility
of an oil sanction, but as described in Chapter 3, the whole
movement for sanctions lost momentum over the winter of 1936
and in July the Co-ordinating Committee met to recommend
that the sanctions be lifted.[22]

Similar problems of implementation were encountered by the UN when sanctions were imposed on Rhodesia. No action had been taken on the proposal of the Collective Measures Committee (set up during the Korean War by the General Assembly under the Uniting for Peace Resolution) for a standing Co-ordinating Committee to plan, evaluate and supervise collective measures, and the sanctions against Rhodesia thus had no institutional back-up. A Commonwealth Sanctions Committee set up in January 1966, following the Lagos Prime Minister's Conference, maintained a general surveillance over trade with Rhodesia, seeking to check evasion by making representations to governments on the basis of information collected by the Commonwealth Secretariat,[23] but it could only perform an unofficial 'watchdog' role.

When mandatory UN sanctions were imposed in December 1966, the Secretary General was asked to report regularly on implementation; in turn, he asked governments to submit monthly returns on a standard form of questionnaire. It was left to each member to devise its own mode of implementation, with no standardised controls or exemption procedures and no independent system of inspection. A Security Council Sanctions Committee was not established until May 1968, when comprehensive sanctions were introduced; its duties were to examine reports from the Secretariat, and to seek information from members about implementation of sanctions and possible sanctions-breaking activities.[24] There were originally seven members of this committee, Britain, France, the United States and USSR and three non-permanent members of the Security Council, but in 1970 it was enlarged to fifteen to include all Security Council members. It held regular, closed meetings and operated by consensus. It received reports of alleged sanctions violations from governments (virtually all from the British government) and (after 1973) from individuals and non-governmental bodies, which it proceeded to investigate by seeking information from governments. The UN Secretariat provided data and statistical material to assist the Committee in its work.

In its eleven years of life the Committee received an average of 50 new cases each year and many continued under investigation over a long period. For instance, in 1977, 342 cases were under consideration. Some governments did not reply to repeated requests for information; others delayed or sent replies which were perfunctory and unenlightening. The network of links operating to handle illegal trade with Rhodesia proved incredibly complex and hard to expose. Apart from a few important cases which were initially brought to light through the detective-work of investigative journalists, the cases dealt with by the Committee represented no more than the tip of the iceberg of sanctions evasion. A manual of documentation and procedures to assist governments in detecting and dealing with sanctions violations was under consideration for some years, but was never compiled.

The Committee considered general issues as well as specific cases; examples of the former being relations with the OAU, closer contacts with non-governmental bodies, and the expansion of sanctions. There was a permanent division of opinion in the Committee between the USSR and third world representatives on the one hand and western representatives on the other in respect of the propriety of forwarding a recommendation to the Security Council for the extension of sanctions to South Africa. Britain and the US saw this as outside the Committee's terms of reference.[25]

The main weapon of the Security Council Committee was publicity; it was powerless to follow up instances of sanctions breaking except by urging governments to do so within their national jurisdictions. Within national administrations, surveillance of sanctions breaking by private business interests was not a high priority and the British government's assiduous reporting of suspected violations to the UN Sanctions Committee, as well as its record of prosecuting some sanctions violators within its own area of jurisdiction, looked a great deal less impressive in the light of the disclosures officially confirmed by the Bingham Report that senior ministers knew, from early in 1968, that oil was reaching Rhodesia through a chain of suppliers which included subsidiaries of BP and Shell.

Nor were all the difficulties a product of governmental foot-dragging. Western democratic governments need the co-operation and consent of the agricultural, industrial and business communities to implement economic and financial sanctions, and they may be unsympathetic or even hostile to politically-inspired restrictive measures. Legal and practical difficulties which can arise between the bureaucratic and business sectors are well illustrated in P. J. Kuyper's study of the Dutch government's effort to carry out its UN obligations for the full implementation of sanctions.[26]

However limited the role of the Security Council Sanctions Committee and the Commonwealth Sanctions Committee, they did provide some monitoring of the collective effort against Rhodesia and achieve some publicising of its shortcomings. Where sanctions have no organisational backing, there is no such procedure and each government is on its own. Nor is it bound by any international legal obligation to restrict dealings with the target and this may reduce its legal competence to do so within its own borders. It may have to rely on the voluntary co-operation of the affected sector, which may not be forthcoming. The Olympic boycott showed how problematical that could be.

8 The Impact of Sanctions

It was noted in the previous chapter that where compliance is the objective the most economical use of sanctions would be the case where a threat was sufficient to induce the target to admit and correct the error of its ways. If sanctions are imposed, cost and dislocation for all will be minimised if speedy compliance follows. But in the cases of sanctions examined in this study the typical response of the target has been negative. Allegations of wrong-doing have not been accepted and a determined effort has been made to resist, circumvent and overcome the effects of deprivation. Even when mandatory sanctions were imposed by the United Nations, the Rhodesian regime rejected its authority.

This is not to claim that sanctions are without political, economic and psychological effects although it is difficult to measure them. Other factors and forces will also be at work and no one knows what the situation would have been in the absence of sanctions. Successful defiance of economic sanctions by the target may actually produce durable, beneficial changes in the structure of its economy. Moreover it is impossible to contain the damage, and sanctions which were intended to have specific negative effects on the target, leaving the rest of the world relatively unscathed, may produce unintended and diffused effects. Changes induced by sanctions in patterns of international commercial and financial interaction may cost the sanctioning group far more than was anticipated, and even trigger an unforeseen and unwelcome chain of events which is difficult to control. In the last chapter the difficulty of estimating cost for the sanctioning states was linked to such factors as objectives and domestic repercussions. In this chapter, the discussion of cost focuses on the impact of collective measures on the target, and on spillover and ripple effects on third states and on the international system.

TARGET IMPACT

Vulnerability to economic sanctions is a function of dependence on external supplies of goods or capital and on external markets for domestic products and to some extent a potential target of sanctions can act in advance to minimise their impact. Even in the Italian case, where it only became clear that sanctions were likely to be imposed a short time before League decisions were taken, Mussolini took a number of anticipatory economic and political measures, including exchange control and an intensive propaganda campaign.[1] Rhodesia was warned in October 1964 that UDI would mean British sanctions and this gave all sectors of the economy a full year to plan and strengthen their defences; in D. G. Clarke's words 'a critical short-term breathing space'.[2] The Republic of South Africa has had more than thirty years to work towards self-sufficiency.

Typical advance action to reduce the effect of trade embargoes includes stockpiling; the development of alternative sources of supply; the stimulation and diversification of domestic production; control of strategic resources, and the development of industrial substitutes. Conservation of foreign exchange is an obvious strategy; improved and diversified transportation systems may be developed to reduce dependence on one outlet. In the wider sphere of inter-state economic relations, new links can be forged through trade agreements and other marketing arrangements. Existing agreements and contracts in process of execution have often been exempted from sanctions. Italy, Iran and Argentina are cases in point. A policy of cultivating friends and neighbours may well pay dividends by reducing the impact of sanctions. Not all of these measures will be available to all governments, but effective planning can be done provided the government can rely on support from politically and economically influential sectors of the population.

If sanctions are imposed, it will be important for the target to minimise their effects. As far as economic sanctions are concerned, its government can probably look confidently for an automatic defensive reaction by adversely affected domestic sectors. The effects of sanctions can be countered by adaptation, reduction of external dependence and possibly the development of new links with non-sanctioning states. Galtung made the point well in noting that a target society can be seen as 'an organism with self maintaining potential. When hit and hurt it reacts – like most organisms – in such a way as to try and undo the damage and to restore the status quo ante.'[3] The target may also be able to take counter-measures to persuade the sanctioning group to get out of the game. Italy, Rhodesia, Iran and Argentina all followed this course of action.

The more comprehensive the sanctions, the greater the effort that will have to be made to evade or endure them. Overcoming a limited grain embargo requires no more than finding an alternative supplier, whereas Rhodesia under comprehensive UN sanctions was in a very precarious position, particularly as it did not gain political recognition for its self-styled independence, even from its best friend and neighbour to the south.

In some instances embargoes on exports to the target state may act as a stimulant to domestic production as the elimination of foreign competition provides a form of protection to local producers. Investment in production for the enlarged home market will become more profitable, and for consumers there will be the added spur of patriotic feeling, encouraging them to buy home-produced goods. A full-scale programme of economic sanctions can have similar effects: by blocking normal channels of supply it may provide a forcing ground for industrial expansion and/or increased agricultural production in the target. All these features were characteristic of the response of Rhodesian domestic industry and Rhodesian consumers under United Nations sanctions. Strack notes that between 1965 and 1975 the volume of manufacturing production in Rhodesia rose 88 per cent and the range of output increased from 802 to 3837 products.[4] Development and diversification in manufacturing, in agriculture and in the processing of agricultural products helped to offset deterioration in certain sectors of the economy, particularly in the tobacco industry.

Another example is South Africa which has been subject to a mandatory UN arms embargo since 1977 and has made great strides in weapons production. It is now the seventh largest arms producer in the world, competing with some of its former suppliers. As noted in Chapter 4, European Community sanctions imposed on South Africa in September 1985 include a ban on imports of military materiel from the Republic. One can also cite the pipeline embargoes which, as pointed out in the EC Note of Protest to the US government in August 1982 provided the Soviets 'with a strong inducement to enlarge their own manufacturing capacity and to accelerate their own turbine and compressor development, thus becoming independent of western sources'.[5]

Where exports from the target are banned, exchange control is certain and import control may also be instituted. Non-essential imports may be prohibited, or drastically restricted, and other imports controlled by a licence–quota system. Quotas may be allocated to importers on a *pro rata* basis, as a percentage of their imports in a normal, pre-crisis year. If necessary, consumer goods can be rationed and consumption held in check by taxation and exhortations to save, backed by the issue of savings bonds. Scarce materials can be allocated to industry on a quota basis; labour may be directed into important jobs; and if sanctions cause unemployment problems, government schemes for maintaining employment may be instituted. Special compensatory action may be taken to assist groups particularly hard hit by sanctions; alternatively the dominant political group may shift some of the impact of sanctions to less privileged groups. For instance, in Rhodesia, it was possible for white employment levels to be protected at the expense of African workers. Monetary and fiscal policy can also be adjusted to counter strains on the economy. All these measures, which correspond broadly to those which are usually imposed by a government in time of war, can be justified in terms of the crisis, particularly if there is a national will to resist sanctions.

Writing on the Italian response to sanctions, M. J. Bonn noted that 'stocks on hand, the practice of economies, the development of substitutes, and the purchase of goods with gold, foreign securities, emigrants' remittances and tourists' disbursements kept the country going without too severe a strain'.[6] The government of Rhodesia used many of the same methods initially with some success. Shortages of consumer goods were experienced, but only petrol was rationed, and the rationing was lifted between 1971 and 1974. Renwick comments that the legacies of sanctions included 'a much more diversified agriculture and the rapid development of manufacturing industry' although the subsistence sector was 'in a desperate plight'.[7]

The second major defensive strategy involves non-participants in sanctions and it will be particularly convenient for the target if they are neighbours and/or powerful enough to give substantial aid. Generalisations are impossible, as circumstances vary from case to case, but the support of other states will always be valuable and may be crucial for the target's survival. Such help has been sought and received by countries subjected to regional economic pressure as well as by Italy under League sanctions and Rhodesia under UN sanctions. In the Falklands crisis Argentina looked to the OAS for support. Yugoslavia, Albania and Cuba all reoriented their trade and sought external aid because of regional pressure and all survived with their governments and policies in place.

Sanctions evasion is a third strategy and here the possibilities are endless. 'Smuggling' becomes highly profitable for middlemen who can charge an inflated commission; in the target state, it will have official blessing if it succeeds in systematically disposing of exports or obtaining imports through clandestine channels. Complicated systems of staged delivery can be worked out, and this process will be made easier if non-participants or friendly countries can be used as intermediate supply points. Where certificates of origin are called for, they can be falsified. One of the major problems in detecting evasion of sanctions by Rhodesia was the use of bills of lading and Chamber of Commerce certificates emanating from South Africa which had to be accepted as sufficient proof of origin. Equally complicated, but no less efficient financial arrangements can be devised to overcome difficulties of payment. The labyrynth of arrangements can become impenetrable. Renwick comments that the evasion of sanctions in Rhodesia became 'routine'.[8]

Commercial interests which have no concern with the objectives of sanctions will only be deterred from the chance to make additional profits or from the prospect of sustaining severe loss if heavy penalties are likely to be incurred and enforced. This presupposes an efficient system of inspection and control within the borders of sanctioning states which is unlikely to be in place.

Financial transactions, like commercial transactions can be passed through a number of intermediaries ('laundered') so that the original sources and the ultimate destination are disguised. The raising of capital for the expansion of the Rhodesian Iron and Steel Corporation (RISCO) plant at QueQue was a case in point; details which came to light after investigation showed the interposition of the South African Steel Corporation (Pty) Ltd between loans arranged by Swiss interests and ultimate recipients.[9]

The Security Council Sanctions Committee on Rhodesia investigated about 350 cases of alleged sanctions evasions between 1968 and 1979 and its reports illustrate graphically the points made above.[10] Similarly the Bingham and Commonwealth Secretariat reports on oil sanctions, to which reference was made in an earlier chapter, showed only too clearly how a helpful neighbour can render export embargoes useless. The British government turned a blind eye to swap arrangements between subsidiaries of Shell and BP in South Africa which permitted the Rhodesian agency GENTA to purchase oil. South Africa was in a position to apply penalties to local companies if they violated South African law; British law required the upholding of UN sanctions. But the British government did not want a confrontation with South Africa. Technically, direct supply was avoided while indirect supply was countenanced; in practical terms the oil sanction was a failure.[11]

The government of a country subjected to sanctions may also impose its own counter-measures. Their effect will vary according to the degree of dependence of sanctioning states on their economic relations with the target, and there may be considerable vulnerability. Assets can be sequestrated and debts repudiated. Italy exacted a belated penalty from the countries which imposed sanctions upon her by meeting financial obligations to post-sanctions creditors before discharging pre-sanctions debts. Soon after UDI Rhodesia blocked payments to residents of Britain, Zambia and the United States and repudiated interest payable on debts to Britain and for which the British government was the guarantor, including a World Bank loan. Britain as the responsible power had to meet these charges. Strack notes that financial counter-sanctions relieved Rhodesia of 'making capital repayments and interest payments on an obligation of about £160 million'.[12] Targets of sanctions can also impose restrictions on trade. Argentina banned some imports from members of the European Community in retaliation for their trade embargoes, while South Africa has threatened to withhold chrome exports if western governments subject it to sanctions.

Expropriation of property is another familiar weapon. The Cuban government nationalised sugar plantations and processing plants, oil refineries, and electric and telephone companies belonging to United States interests as a declared reprisal for the cut in the sugar quota; this led to a total embargo on trade with Cuba being imposed by the United States.

Increased domestic opposition to the target government, not

consolidation of support for it, is normally an objective of group sanctions. This may be the product of hardship which the economic sanctions impose; it may also result from diplomatic and cultural penalties and from sensitivity to international condemnation. But it is by no means a certain outcome; instead there may be a heightened sense of solidarity and national purpose, particularly if core values (such as national unity and pride or even white supremacy) are at stake. Such intense feelings are unlikely to be paralleled in the sanctioning states. The expected impact on public opinion in the target may also be softened or lost because its citizens are not fully aware of the issues or able to make an accurate judgement of the situation. Government control of the media in a closed society such as the Soviet Union makes it difficult for outside messages to be received; it is doubtful if the partial boycott of the Moscow Olympics was understood by all Soviet citizens to be a penalty for Afghanistan.

The point is also worth making that sanctions can not only help leaders to present themselves as effective defenders of the country and its people from external enemies,[13] but can also provide them with a useful explanation for any economic difficulties or setbacks which may be encountered, whether or not there is any connection. It is often difficult to distinguish between or to identify sources of economic difficulty, but always convenient to blame them on outside agencies. In Cuba, in Rhodesia, and most recently in Poland, sanctions have been so blamed.

A government determined to resist sanctions will obviously take positive steps to rally public opinion behind its policy of non-compliance. Public morale will be crucial and can be bolstered by skilful propaganda. Willingness to make sacrifices and adapt to shortages, commonly associated with a war effort, will be fostered by the government and instead of economic deprivation undermining its position it may strengthen it. A siege psychosis, once engendered, can be a powerful factor in sustaining the will to resist and it will enable the government to take unpopular measures such as rationing consumer goods.[14] There is a danger too, that this defiant reaction may mean less readiness to compromise than before sanctions were imposed, so that a peaceful solution of the crisis becomes more and not less difficult to achieve. This may affect both sanctioning and sanctioned: the former, committed to a policy of coercion, may demand unrealistic concessions to justify the termination of sanctions, while concessions by the target government may appear as a betrayal of national values to its citizens. If the issues appear clear cut, and national feeling has been roused in support of resistance to sanctions, compromise will look like defeat, and it will be difficult for the government of the country to adopt a more conciliatory attitude without loss of face.

One of the most interesting features of the League sanctions experiment was the extent to which the Italian people rallied behind Mussolini. Baer notes that 'what was meant to be only instrumental economic pressure to elicit internal protest was transformed by the Italian government into a cause for rapid intensification of integral economic and political nationalism ... sanctions made the Ethiopian war popular'.[15]

In post-war programmes of economic denial, the typical reaction has been defiance. Popular support for leadership was notable in Yugoslavia, Albania and Cuba where sanctions could be presented as unwarranted interference with national independence. It is true that the Arab oil embargo appeared to 'work' against Western Europe and particularly against Japan but this required no more than a foreign policy shift without threat to internal values. The United States reaction was much sharper and there was no question of it abandoning Israel as an ally. Indeed, counter-measures, such as military action and food boycotts were openly discussed and Israel was guaranteed oil imports.[16]

Issues are of course more complex where the target's population is openly divided on the merits of the offending policy, whether foreign or domestic. Rhodesia in the late 1960s and 1970s and South Africa to this day are obviously special cases. While whites have a vested interest in the status quo one can hardly expect the black population to rally in defence of white minority rule. Although there had been opposition to a unilateral declaration of independence among white Rhodesians, once UDI was declared there was a general willingness to try and make it work and a high level of white morale was maintained, with the Smith regime making special and successful efforts to protect white interests under sanctions. There was also misplaced confidence that sanctions would eventually wither away or be lifted. As time passed, the steady increase in the scale of guerrilla activity inside the country was demoralising, as was the erosion of South African support, and it can also be assumed that the psychic effects of international isolation and total non-recognition of Rhodesia as an independent state took their toll. Outnumbered twenty to one by blacks, white Rhodesians began to emigrate in large numbers, principally to South Africa. The Smith government initiated serious negotiations for majority rule in 1976. Black Rhodesians had shown in their rejection of the proposals put to them by the Pearce Commission that they were intent on a real, and not a nominal transfer of power; for them, the UN sanctions underlined the legitimacy of their cause even if they also contributed to personal economic hardship.

For 'pariah' states like Rhodesia and South Africa the impact of world condemnation cannot be discounted. In particular, exclusion from international organisations effectively deprives their governments of an important forum in which to present their own case and answer charges made by those who condemn them. South African whites have nowhere to turn but the west, because their regional neighbours are hostile to their policies. If the western world turns against them, their isolation will be intense and it will not mean security in some remote location but insecurity in the midst of a hostile, oppressed black population.

IMPACT ON THIRD PARTIES

The effects of economic sanctions are not limited to the parties directly involved. Inevitably third parties will also be affected. In some cases they may be beneficiaries: Argentina sold grain to the USSR to make up the shortfall caused by the US embargo in 1980; Turkey has been named as the chief beneficiary of Arab League trade embargoes against Egypt in 1979.[17] There are profits to be made by bystander states in any sanctions exercise which does not have universal support. These windfall gains will be resented by sanctioning states and will prompt attempts on their part to persuade third parties not to fill the gaps left by sanctions but to maintain normal trade with the target. In the past such efforts have not enjoyed much success.

Of more concern, however, are cases where third states are seriously affected by sanctions on their neighbours or trading partners. Article 50 of the UN Charter provides that any member or non-member who faces 'special economic problems' as a result of UN preventive or enforcement measures 'shall have the right to consult the Security Council with regard to a solution of these problems'. In Article 49, members pledge mutual assistance in carrying out such measures. These are skeletal provisions, but they do provide a basis for claims from adversely affected states. In the case of sanctions against Rhodesia, a heavy burden was placed on some of Rhodesia's neighbours, particularly Zambia and post-independence Mozambique. These countries, with Botswana and Tanzania, found themselves in the 'front-line' because of sanctions and of their support for guerrilla forces seeking to overthrow the white regime.[18]

Zambia was particularly hard hit being generally oriented southwards to Rhodesia, Mozambique and South Africa. The copper mines which were the mainstay of the economy (providing over 90 per cent of foreign earnings) depended on Rhodesian coal which was carried by Rhodesian railways; the same railways carried copper to the coast for shipment and provided Zambia's main transport link with the outside world. Rail and air services were jointly owned and operated until June 1967; the Beira–Umtali pipeline served both countries; the jointly owned Kariba hydro-electric project was situated in Rhodesia. Furthermore, Zambia was accustomed to importing about one-third of her total imports from Rhodesia and 94 per cent from Rhodesia and South Africa together. Alternative road transportation routes were unsatisfactory and the Benguela Railway to Lobito Bay was closed in 1975 during the Angolan civil war. Zambia closed its border with Rhodesia in 1973, but was forced to reopen it in 1978 or face a total collapse of the Zambian economy. The Tazara railway linking the copperbelt and Dar-es-Salaam, built with Chinese aid and completed in 1976, could not handle the traffic, and Dar itself was choked with shipping.[19]

Problems were compounded by the dramatic fall in copper prices between 1974 and 1975, which could not be attributed to sanctions or the liberation struggle, but other strains were clearly the direct result of attempts to develop self-sufficiency, (for instance, hydro-electric projects) and to diversify trade which meant higher priced imports as well as new transport routes. Not only were some of these enterprises likely to be redundant if and when a political settlement was reached in Rhodesia but local and foreign investment declined because political and economic uncertainties militated against risk-taking.

Tanzania was less seriously affected, but the provision of transport facilities for Zambia constituted a heavy burden; Botswana was rendered more dependent on South Africa (as indeed were Zambia and Mozambique). Mozambique closed its border with Rhodesia and imposed sanctions in March 1976 and lost foreign exchange and jobs as a result. Resources which were needed for reconstruction after the liberation struggle had to be diverted to other purposes.

These costs to the Front Line States cannot be separated from the costs of supporting guerrilla bases and accommodating refugees – who became more numerous once the forces of the Patriotic Front began to make serious incursions into Rhodesian territory. But some estimates were made of the cost of sanctions in the early stages of the programme: the former Co-ordinator of UN assistance to Zambia, Sir Robert Jackson, attributed $100 million expenditure to the consequences of UDI and the decision to apply sanctions in the period 1965–8.[20] In the next three years (1969–72), at least an equivalent amount was spent; between 1972 and 1977, $744 million. Estimates of costs to Mozambique of applying sanctions were also made by UN missions. In the first year 1975–6, direct costs were put at $139–$165 million and thereafter at about $110–$135 million per annum.[21] Losses stemmed from earnings of migrant workers, substitutes for Rhodesian facilities and an increased trade deficit.

Economic sanctions against Rhodesia placed a heavy burden on the struggling economies of these neighbouring states, which already faced appalling problems of underdevelopment, illiteracy, lack of industrial base and public services, not to mention their susceptibility to natural disasters such as floods and droughts. And while it is true that their support for the armed struggle in Rhodesia increased this burden, violence was not their chosen instrument for change. The Lusaka Manifesto, adopted in 1969, but peaceful methods first.

It is clear that comprehensive sanctions which dislocate existing patterns of economic activity can bear as heavily on innocent neighbours as on the delinquent target; as discussed further in

Chapter 9, if South Africa is subjected to international sanctions, its key role in the overall economic life of the region would mean that neighbouring states would inevitably suffer adverse consequences which could only be partially offset by UN or Commonwealth aid.

In the Rhodesian case the UN responded to a limited degree with assistance for Zambia, Botswana and Mozambique. The Commonwealth also gave help to these states, including Mozambique which is not a member of the Commonwealth. Where there is no framework of international organisation for sanctions, formal claims for compensation or support by adversely affected third states are ruled out. It is unlikely that those who would be seriously harmed will join in, unless the penalties for not doing so are perceived as likely to be greater.

Costs to the sanctioning states, to targets and to third states must all be expected in any major collective sanctions endeavour; system damage is a further concern. The inter-connectedness of the world economy and its vulnerability to disruption of commercial and financial flows has been fully demonstrated over the last decade, beginning with the quadrupling of oil prices and the Arab oil embargoes in the early 1970s. It is obvious that if major economic powers resort to economic weapons of foreign policy for any reason, there are likely to be repercussions throughout the system. The United States is a dominant influence in world markets, and Western Europe and Japan are also major centres of economic power. Inter-relationships between OECD countries, and between OECD countries and the developing world, are so close that shock effects are transmitted throughout the whole network and may gain momentum as they travel along fault lines, while trade and credit relations between Western Europe and the Eastern European countries, plus the Soviet Union, have grown steadily in recent years and are now susceptible to mutual damage. In addition, western bank lending on a lavish scale both to Latin American and East European governments has heightened the vulnerability of the international financial system.

It is even more difficult to predict systemic effects of sanctions than the effects they may have on their targets. Intangible factors, particularly confidence, may be crucial particularly where aid and investment are concerned. In periods of instability, there will be reluctance to make things worse and the dangers of triggering ripple effects which are uncontrollable and destabilising, may make governments very reluctant to embark on politically motivated economic penalties.[22]

The catalogue of woes besetting the international economy since the mid 1970s is well known: inflation, unemployment, recession in the OECD countries; agricultural failure, low productivity and inflation in the Soviet Union and Eastern Europe; loss of foreign exchange earning capacity and massive debt in the Third World, compounding existing problems of poverty and overpopulation.

Systemic effects which need to be reckoned with, particularly in such hard times, can be of various kinds and a number of examples can be given. Iranian assets were frozen by the United States in the Tehran hostages crisis, and this was certainly inconvenient for Iran. Claims were immediately lodged against these frozen assets by American creditors of Iran and so a negotiated settlement became inevitable. But what if this action had produced a loss of confidence in the security of deposits in western banks and led to massive withdrawals of petro-dollar deposits? This concern was expressed by the US State Department which initially opposed the freeze. Some OPEC members did move deposits to non-American banks and Marshall Goldman pointed out that although the United States 'has enormous leverage at its disposal ... once a lever is pulled there is an ever-decreasing likelihood that the US can pull that lever again'.[23] He labelled this the 'Iranian Deposit Syndrome'. Lissakers suggests that although the results of the asset freeze may not have been as 'dire' as predicted, the 'psychology of the Euro-currency market has changed and ... Eurodollars have unquestionably become more politicized'.[24]

An even more alarming scenario arose from the international debt crisis; it involved the danger of a series of defaults by major debtors which could spell disaster for the international banking system. For this reason, Poland – a major debtor – could not be treated too harshly even by the United States; in 1982 it owed $16 000 million to western banks. Argentina – another major debtor – was also spared the full rigours of financial sanctions. In fact Britain and Argentina reciprocally lifted financial sanctions (but not trade sanctions) in mid-September 1982 in order to allow Argentina to meet some of the capital and interest payments due before the end of the year on its $34 billion foreign debt, of which $26 billion was bank debt. Assets frozen in Britain amounted to $1.4 billion and this deterred bankers in other centres from lending more funds to Argentina.[25] The fear of default or repudiation was widespread in the international banking community which was also faced with mountainous debts in other countries, for instance Mexico, Romania and Hungary.

Exacerbating East–West relations can have negative security implications; exacerbating North–South tensions is counterproductive in welfare terms. And even UN sanctions can have dangerous ripple effects which are felt throughout the international system. Systemic political effects may also be generated locally or regionally by political and economic sanctions. Forcing Cuba into greater dependence on the Soviet Union may have had implications for the use of Cuban forces in Africa; driving Poland to integrate more closely with the Soviet bloc was hardly one of the West's objectives in imposing economic penalties for martial law and the outlawing of Solidarity. It is generally accepted that Rhodesian UDI produced a closer relationship with South Africa which it is difficult, if not impossible for the Zimbabwean government to reverse. The particular problems which could accompany full-scale economic sanctions against South Africa are discussed in the next chapter.

9 The Case of South Africa

Chapter 4, which dealt with United Nations sanctions, sketched the record of the UN in regard to South Africa up to the end of 1985 and noted that as a result of heightened concern about deteriorating race relations in the Republic, and with the encouragement of Security Council Resolution 569, the United States, European Community and Commonwealth members imposed some political and economic sanctions in the autumn of that year. US measures banned the export of computers for use by the South African security forces as well as exports of nuclear goods and technology (except as required by IAEA rules on health and safety); prohibited most government loans to the South African government; and proposed a ban on the import of Krugerrands. EC measures ended military co-operation and banned new collaboration in nuclear sectors; banned the export of oil to South Africa and the export of sensitive equipment for use by the South African police; discouraged cultural agreements and froze sporting and security links. Commonwealth sponsored measures were similar to those imposed by the United States.

The three major grounds for sanctions against South Africa have been its assistance to the illegal regime in Rhodesia, its continued control of Namibia and the system of apartheid itself. The first of these is now a dead issue, but the second and third are very much alive. In the past two years there has been a new surge of antipathy in the West to the philosophy and practice of apartheid, coinciding with internal unrest and demonstrations against the South African regime which have been countered with a marked degree of police brutality. In 1985 the turmoil in black townships, and the efforts by the security forces to suppress it, received extensive television coverage in North America and Europe. Eventually the South African government banned journalists and camera crews from the townships, but the films seen night after night in their living rooms had vividly brought home to many people in the west the poverty and degradation of African living conditions as well as the strength of opposition to apartheid and the ruthless methods of repression used by the security forces. As the loss of life grew greater, the international Anti-Apartheid movement pressed harder for sanctions: on the one hand as a response to a totally unacceptable system being prolonged by totally unacceptable means, and on the other with the hope that white South Africans' resolve was at last beginning to crumble so that intensified external pressure could hasten the process of change. In other words, those advocating comprehensive sanctions were expecting them to have coercive as well as expressive and punitive effects.

The measures actually imposed by western governments in 1985 were very mild; banning the export of computers to the South African security forces, or the import of Krugerrands, could not be considered drastic punishment. But in symbolic terms these measures were important as they represented a qualitative shift in western governmental policy which was certainly not welcome to the South African government. By the autumn of 1985 it was also obvious that 'private sanctions' were having a visible effect. US banks became nervous about their involvement with South Africa and refused to renew short-term loans, while public pressure in the United States and Canada was also having an influence on corporate attitudes. In September the South African government was faced with a serious fall in the value of the rand and declared a moratorium on foreign debt repayment to allow for rescheduling negotiations. At the same time there were signs of changing attitudes in the Republic. Blacks were becoming more militant in confronting the security forces and were beginning to turn against fellow blacks who were – or were thought to be – co-operating with the authorities. More encouraging for the prospect of peaceful change was the visit of the chairman of the giant Anglo–American Corporation and some of his senior executives to Lusaka to have discussions with the exiled and outlawed leaders of the African National Congress.[1] Less encouraging was the government's willingness to talk about change but failure to do much about it, thereby increasing the level of frustration inside and outside the country. In August 1985 President Botha dashed expectations that he would introduce a time table for specific and significant reforms and his speech at the opening of the South African Parliament in January 1986 promised revision, not abolition of influx control, and a 'start' to involvement of black communities in decision making beyond the local government level.[2]

As all those who are concerned with South Africa are aware, the literature on the subject is enormous and there are many detailed studies of the internal political, economic and social problems faced by South Africa as well as of its foreign policy.[3] The question of sanctions has also been extensively analysed and debated although, as might be expected, estimates of the effects and the effectiveness of different measures differ widely.[4] This chapter can do no more than present the major considerations which are relevant to the issue of sanctions, drawing on expert studies and on experience with other cases discussed in earlier chapters.

There is no controversy over the unacceptability of the South African system which on the one hand denies equality of status and political participation to the majority of its citizens, discriminating solely on grounds of skin colour, and on the other treats demands for fundamental change as criminal offences. The whole body of United Nations work in the field of human rights leaves little doubt that institutionalised racial discrimination violates international law as well as international morality, and there is unanimity in the UN, as in the Commonwealth, that there is international responsibility to address the South African problem. Namibia's right to self determination and independence has also been fully established at the international level. The grounds for international action are therefore quite clear and this in itself makes the South African case unique.

Nor is there any dispute about the character of non-violent measures imposed on South Africa. Whether mandatory (under Security Council order) or voluntary, these measures are indisputably international sanctions: penalties for behaviour which is not in conformity with standards which have come to be universally accepted. This does not mean that South Africa is the only country whose government falls short of fulfilling international obligations; it does mean that there is a (rare) consensus that the particularly blatant form of racial discrimination and persecution which has come to be known as apartheid is unacceptable and must sooner or later be eliminated. The last chapter of this book examines the implications of failure to deal firmly and consistently with other acts of wrong-doing, as well as the undue 'stretching' of the sanctions label to cover acts which would more correctly be described as reprisals or economic coercion of a self-serving nature. Here we confront the particular problem of what to do about South Africa, which is an important issue for the international community as a whole but especially for the west because significant external economic pressure can only come from western sources.

The disagreement which bedevils the issue is therefore not what is wrong with South Africa, but how to put it right, and reflects doubts and uncertainties about the likely consequences of different forms of pressure. The ambivalence of official western opinion on this score was accurately reflected in Security Council Resolution 569 which trenchantly condemned apartheid, and the South African government's failure to take meaningful steps towards political reform, and at the same time left it to members of the United Nations to take such measures as they find appropriate.

There is, of course, a wide spectrum of opinion outside South Africa about the best course of action. At one extreme are most Third World governments and the Anti-Apartheid Movement, which has strong support from political, labour and religious groups throughout the Western world, who favour the total isolation of South Africa by severing all economic, cultural and communications ties. The Republic has already been effectively excluded from participation in most international organisations. The objective of this 'excommunication' is to make the continuation of present policies impossible and to usher in a new political dispensation on the basis of universal franchise as quickly as possible. The ban on sporting contacts which dates from the late 1970s and brought an end to segregation in the South African sporting world is cited as evidence of what can be achieved by a concerted boycott,[5] while severance of direct air links with the Republic is also widely canvassed as an effective measure. For many years the advocates of economic sanctions emphasised oil as the Republic's Achilles heel; an embargo on oil sales to South Africa, which has no indigenous oil resources, was propounded as a means of bringing the economy to a halt. In recent years, however, emphasis has shifted to financial sanctions, particularly disinvestment, as having the best chance of forcing the pace of change. These options are discussed further below.

At the other extreme of opinion are the proponents of what the Reagan Administration labelled 'constructive engagement'. The idea is that economic contacts and dialogue are more likely to be productive of reform than the severance of ties.

Economic growth is seen as a force for good which leads to increased employment, upward mobility and a better standard of living for Africans and other non-white groups in South Africa which will inevitably increase their bargaining power and ensure them an increased role in political life. This route is seen as less revolutionary and therefore less disruptive than the application of harsh sanctions; gradualism will allow a continuous process of adjustment and avoid a breakdown in economic and political life which could have disastrous consequences not only for the people of South Africa of whatever colour, but for neighbouring states who depend on South Africa for their livelihood, as well as for South Africa's trading partners in the west. Western governments and business leaders have generally adopted this stance, and the idea of codes of conduct for branches or subsidiaries of multi-national corporations operating in South Africa has been an offshoot. The European Community introduced such a code for European firms in 1977 (superseding an earlier British code): it requires such firms to issue an annual report on their progress in applying the principles it sets out – which include support for black trade unions, alleviation of the effects of migrant labour, the payment of decent wages and application of the principle of equal pay for equal work.[6] In the United States the Sullivan principles established a voluntary code of conduct for American firms; these principles set out similar guidelines but there was no governmental sponsorship or involvement until President Reagan's executive order of September 1985 which denied US government export assistance to firms operating in South Africa which had not signed the code by the end of the year.[7]

When President Reagan took office in 1980 'constructive engagement' became official policy and Chester Crocker the new Assistant Secretary of State for African Affairs, took charge of its implementation. His views on the correct policy posture towards South Africa had been published in an article in *Foreign Affairs* shortly before he took office: from this it was clear that Namibia was a key element in the strategy which was generally 'to steer between the twin dangers of abetting violence in the

Republic and aligning ... with the cause of white rule'.[8] South African withdrawal from Namibia was to be linked to Cuban withdrawal from Angola, thus achieving two foreign policy goals for the United States. It must be acknowledged in early 1986 that developments over the past five years do not encourage any optimism that this strategy is working.

Between these two extremes there is a considerable middle ground occupied by supporters of a blend of carrots and sticks as well as carrotless stick-wielders and stick-wavers. The trend at the time of writing is away from constructive engagement towards firmer pressure. The hardening of attitudes in the autumn of 1985 reflects, at least in part, a concern that if nothing is done about South Africa not only will leading powers in the West be identified as tolerant, if not supportive, of apartheid, thus forfeiting any claim to respect, but that things will go from bad to worse in the Republic with a steady escalation of violence perhaps ending in a bloodbath. Ensuing anarchy would be disastrous for all South Africans and would leave the West little hope of influencing the future course of events.

The South African government's new constitutional arrangements introduced in 1984 are clearly no answer to the problem. The total black population which now numbers about 25 million (including those living in the homelands) compared with 5 million whites, is given no role or representation in the central government and although legislative chambers have been introduced for South Africa's three million Coloured people and one million Asians, the fact that less than 20 per cent of eligible Coloured and Asian voters participated in the election of representatives was a clear indication that credibility is lacking. The African National Congress, which is banned within the Republic's borders, officially supports sanctions from its headquarters in Zambia and claims that the majority of black South Africans are prepared to suffer any hardships sanctions may entail as part of the price of emancipation. On the other hand Chief Buthelezi, leader of the Zulu movement Inkatha, who rejected 'independence' for Kwazulu declares himself to be opposed to economic sanctions on the grounds that they would do great damage to African interests, and other polls also suggest African opposition.[9] Within South Africa it is an offence to advocate sanctions and this obviously acts as a brake on the free expression of views whether by the United Democratic

Front, which was formed as a reaction to the new constitution, or by others representing African interests. The issue of sanctions is inevitably linked with the acceptability of violence as a means of bringing change. Nelson Mandela, who was imprisoned for life in 1964 for organising violent protest, and who enjoys a unique status as a symbol of African resistance and a potential national leader, has been offered his freedom by the Botha government on condition that he renounces violence; this he has steadfastly refused to do. The increasing frustration of urban blacks in South Africa, and the obduracy of the South African government can only encourage both resort to violence and support for sanctions. For example, Bishop Tutu who has considerable standing as a Nobel Peace prizewinner and champion of black rights both inside and outside South Africa, openly advocates sanctions.

On the other hand whites are generally, and predictably, opposed to sanctions and even those at the more liberal end of the spectrum of white opinion would prefer the western world to limit its pressure on South Africa to diplomatic forms.[10]

The important question, of course, is what kind of change the peoples of South Africa themselves can agree upon. For blacks change must be far-reaching, otherwise they will reject it just as Africans in Rhodesia rejected the constitutional proposals put to them by the Pearce Commission in 1972. For many whites, change is probably best limited to the minimum needed to avert a breakdown in social order and they would expect safeguards for their minority position in any new constitutional arrangement. Asians and Coloured people are also likely to want safeguards in a black-ruled state. A peaceful and lasting settlement would obviously require complex and protracted negotiations; the danger is polarisation in which moderates of whatever colour are swept aside leaving no room for dialogue.[11]

The problem remains as to what the West should do, and the 'West' in this context means those countries with whom South Africa has major commercial and financial links, namely Britain, the United States, West Germany and France. Complete isolation of South Africa on the model originally set out in Article 16 of the League Covenant is clearly unrealistic as a policy option. So is military intervention in present circumstances. Constructive engagement is now largely discredited.[12]

There remains a wide range of possible sanctions which could be adopted unilaterally or on a collective basis, and it may be useful to follow the sequence of discussion in Chapters 7 and 8 to explore the dimensions of these policy choices.

The basic question is that of motive or objective: what western governments really hope to achieve. If they are concerned only to send signals of disapproval which at the same time pre-empt demands for stronger measures – whether these demands come from internal sources (as in the United States) or from external sources (as with Commonwealth pressure on Britain) coercive measures can be ruled out. This was certainly the message conveyed both by the US Secretary of State and the British Prime Minister in their (separate) statements to the press in the autumn of 1985. However, this state of affairs can only give cold comfort to the South African government because moral and prudential concerns could produce further shifts in government policy in the United States – and in Britain – so that harsher measures seem appropriate. If the objective does become that of injuring or crippling the South African economy with the hope that the government will become more amenable to internal reform and power-sharing, experience suggests that relevant considerations for western governments would be costs, target vulnerability and the need for a co-ordinated effort.

It would certainly be foolish to suppose that costs to domestic economies would not be an influential element in sanctioning decisions. Particularly for Britain, and to a lesser extent for all South Africa's major trading partners, the loss of export markets could mean the loss of jobs at home as well as of foreign exchange earnings. More serious, perhaps, would be the loss of important minerals which South Africa exports and for which, in some cases, the only alternative supplier is the Soviet Union. Cutting financial links could also be costly to domestic economies, especially in Britain and West Germany. It is worth looking briefly at trade and investment patterns to assess the significance of the costs of economic and financial sanctions as well as South Africa's vulnerability to them.

Although there can be no certainty about the precise economic effects of particular sanctions on particular sectors of the South African economy and different studies offer different estimates, there is overall agreement inside and outside the Republic that it is vulnerable to interference with foreign trade and foreign investment, both of which are important elements in sustaining – and improving – production, consumption and employment levels.[13] There has been a slight decline in the significance of foreign trade in recent years but in 1982 imports of merchandise and services were equivalent to 32 per cent of GDP (and expenditure on services grew at an annual rate of 15.4 per cent between 1975 and 1981 and continues to grow) while exports were equivalent to 28 per cent of GDP. This is a very high ratio compared with that of other western industrialised countries.

As far as imports are concerned, the Republic's main vulnerability, which could not easily be overcome by import substitution, is in capital and intermediate goods which constitute 80 per cent of the value of total imports. Machinery, vehicles, chemicals and plastics are all important items, as well as oil which is discussed further below. South Africa's major suppliers, ranked in terms of the percentage of imports they supplied in 1984, are West Germany, the United States, Japan, Britain and France; in that year they accounted for approximately 60 per cent of all disclosed imports.[14] Britain's share has declined and is now 11 per cent of the total compared with about 16 per cent for West Germany and the United States and 13 per cent for Japan. In 1982 the United Kingdom South Africa Trade Association (UKSATA) estimated that British exports to South Africa were worth approximately £1300 million per annum and that if this trade were banned approximately 70 000 British jobs would be lost. In addition invisible items (insurance, shipping and other services as well as profits and dividends) were worth approximately £1780 million and re-exports of gold and diamonds accounted for £400 million, giving a total annual value of British earnings from trade with South Africa of £3480 million.[15]

South Africa's export trade is less concentrated in destination, although exports to the rest of Africa have been declining as a percentage of the total value of exports in recent years. Preliminary figures for disclosed exports (excluding gold) in 1984 show the United States as South Africa's best customer, taking 8.3 per cent of exports, followed by Japan (7.7 per cent), Switzerland (6.6 per cent), Britain (4.2 per cent), West Germany (3.9 per cent) and Africa (3.5 per cent).[16] Gold is a major item in the South African balance of payments: on average it accounted for 30 per cent of foreign exchange earnings in the period 1975–81 and in the 1980s the percentage has been even higher, rising to 47 per cent in 1984.[17] South Africa is the world's leading gold producer, accounting for 70 per cent of non-Communist production. Even at a lower price, gold is obviously a crucial factor, and any rise in the gold price benefits the balance of payments as well as the economy as a whole. Other important mineral exports are manganese, chrome, vanadium, platinum and uranium. Together gold and minerals account for over 70 per cent of South Africa's exports. The other major export is agricultural produce which constituted 14 per cent of all merchandise exports (excluding gold) in the period 1975–80. These exports are important in providing employment, particularly for blacks and coloured people, as well as in earning foreign exchange; and there are forward and backward links to other industries which are also significant employers.[18]

The major problem in placing embargoes on South Africa's exports is the dependence of the west, particularly its chemical, steel and aerospace industries, on South African minerals.[19] South Africa and the Soviet Union provide 93 per cent of the west's imports of platinum, 67 per cent of vanadium, 57 per cent of manganese and 55 per cent of chrome. Chrome and platinum are particularly important: a West German government report estimated in 1985 that if chrome imports were reduced by 30 per cent for one year, West Germany's GNP would fall by 25 per cent,[20] while UKSATA has forecast that without South Africa's platinum, 'much of Britain's industry could be brought to a standstill'.[21] Stockpiling has not been undertaken on a serious scale[22] and alternative suppliers are not readily available. The experience of the Byrd Amendment under which the United States imported chrome from Rhodesia for several years in violation of mandatory UN sanctions does not encourage optimism about the popularity or effectiveness of embargoes on South African mineral exports. And even if embargoes are limited to exports from sanctioning states to South Africa, South Africa could conceivably apply controls to its mineral exports as a counter-measure and has threatened to do so. It should also be noted that South Africa has become the world's fourth largest coal exporter – and France's main supplier.

On balance, export embargoes are more credible than import

embargoes and in the past there has been great emphasis on oil as a key commodity suitable for sanctions.[23] South Africa has no indigenous oil resources – and in spite of costly and diligent government-sponsored exploration has not found any – and in the 1960s it was almost entirely dependent on imports. The South African government, of course, was well aware of this vulnerability. Oil has been designated a strategic commodity and no information is published about oil supplies or reserves. As early as 1965 major oil companies were instructed to build up a stockpile, which may now be equivalent to three years' supply. 'Tank farms' were built in Natal and the Cape Province and disused mines are also used for storage. In addition, there are now three government-owned SASOL (oil from coal) plants in operation. In 1981 a UN study estimated that South Africa used 320 000 barrels of oil per day; SASOL could now be producing one half of this amount.[24] Other strategies include reliance on alternative energy sources: in particular South Africa has abundant coal supplies which supply SASOL and are used for generating electricity.

It has been estimated that by 1981 oil accounted for only 25 per cent of South Africa's total energy needs[25] and if a serious shortage developed rationing could also be introduced.

Until 1979 South Africa obtained most of its oil from Iran and was therefore not seriously affected by the embargo imposed by Arab oil-exporting countries in 1973, but after the fall of the Shah, Iran joined in the boycott and since then South Africa has had to obtain oil on the 'spot' market at premium prices. The fall in oil prices in 1986 will relieve this particular pressure on the South African balance of payments, but in any case it no longer seems likely that an oil boycott could bring dramatic results, even if it were universally enforced which is extremely unlikely. A blockade of South African ports – which offer supply and repair services to between 16 000 and 20 000 ships each year – would certainly be needed to accomplish this, as well as the full co-operation of all neighbouring states who are very vulnerable to South African counter-sanctions.

In respect of other items on South Africa's import list, a certain amount of import substitution would undoubtedly occur; where this was difficult or impossible, there would be hardship for the South African economy. However, in discussion of sanctions in recent years emphasis has shifted to financial measures as the most effective means of causing economic distress and thus political change. South Africa has always relied heavily on foreign capital and has suffered from its flight, as happened after Sharpeville in 1960 and again after the Soweto disturbances in 1976. This reliance has not decreased: as Jesmond Blumenfeld points out, foreign capital brings needed technology, helps to provide employment and supports the balance of payments.[26] A low gold price and highly-priced imports make this role even more important.

There is no doubt that campaigns for disinvestment in North America, allied to uncertainties about the future political stability of the Republic which have made private banks unwilling to grant new loans, have seriously affected South Africa's credit standing. Pressure has mounted in the United States to make banks and multi-nationals cut their connections with South Africa. In 1985 the Free South Africa Movement, supported by politicians at all levels of government, the labour movement, churches, students and civil rights groups, achieved notable results in focusing public attention on the South African question, which, in turn, was translated into Congressional proposals for sanctions which President Reagan could not ignore. The campaign for disinvestment has been strong enough to make it preferable for some US companies to sell off their South African interests and for banks to cease doing business with South Africa rather than forfeit domestic business with universities, pension funds and other important investors. It also spares them what has become known as the 'hassle factor.'[27] A growing number of states and municipalities in the United States have now distanced themselves from South African investment and no doubt new investment has been discouraged. As noted earlier in this chapter, media coverage of the unrest in black townships in South Africa helped to fuel public outrage and in the autumn of 1985 a series of US bank moves out of private loans to South Africa precipitated a loss of confidence and a sharp fall in the value of the rand. The South African government promptly reinstituted two-tier exchange controls and imposed a moratorium on all short-term foreign debt repayment. This staved off any spread of the panic to European banks and gave time for negotiation of rescheduling which was reported to be completed through Swiss and other European banks in March 1986. This may suggest that a more pragmatic line is likely in Europe than in North America. For instance, of South Africa's overall foreign debt of $18.5 billion at the end of 1984, Britain holds $5.5 billion and West Germany at least $2 billion. Much of this lending is related to trade. British investment has been estimated to account for approximately 50 per cent of total foreign investment in South Africa; South Africa accounts for nearly 10 per cent of all British overseas direct investment.[28] The market value of this investment was estimated at about £5000 million in 1982; to this must be added about £6000 million of indirect (portfolio) investment.[29] 1200 British companies operate in South Africa compared with 350 West German and 340 US companies. Britain's stake is obviously so large that its participation in sanctions would be crucial; by the same token, its reluctance to join in would be very hard to overcome.

The case for disinvestment has strong moral overtones reflecting the view that business should not be involved with a system built on inequality and injustice; in practical terms it is extremely hard to judge what the effects might be.[30] Physical assets cannot be repatriated and their sale to South African (or non-sanctionist) interests would not necessarily achieve a great deal. Disinvestment does raise the spectre of increased unemployment in South Africa which is already a serious problem for the black community, and benefits from existing EC and US Codes of practice could also be lost. On the other hand, the loss of confidence which would follow major implementation of disinvestment policies might be influential in precipitating change. It is obviously impossible to do justice to the arguments for and against disinvestment in a few paragraphs; for purposes of a general review of the South African sanctions debate it may be agreed that financial sanctions whether privately sponsored or governmentally ordered would undoubtedly hurt the South African economy, as would export embargoes on capital goods. Major issues for western governments considering such measures are whether unity could be preserved among them to avoid serious gaps in the sanctions net; whether South Africa has sufficient defensive strengths to render embargoes generally ineffective; whether the damage to South Africa's neighbours and perhaps to the whole international trade and payments system would be so great that the exercise became self-defeating; and finally whether whatever hurt is inflicted will, in fact, achieve worthwhile results in political terms. Each of these issues deserves some consideration.

In regard to the prospects of solidarity among sanctioning states, the record in other cases is not encouraging. Certainly the United States which has taken a leadership role in many recent sanctions efforts may be prepared to go even further in punishing South Africa than it has done so far. Pressure from domestic groups will continue and may increase, although any Administration will also have to consider the global interests of the United States in respect of South Africa's geopolitical importance in the Southern hemisphere, dominating the sea routes around the Cape.

It seems unlikely, however, that Britain and West Germany will be easily persuaded to adopt severe sanctions. Britain may be less responsive to Commonwealth pressure than it was over Rhodesia; after all, South Africa is not its *constitutional* responsibility and it has much greater economic interests at stake. It can certainly use its veto power to block UN mandatory sanctions. Even with such an order, universality of sanctions implementation would be hard to achieve. Switzerland has already indicated that it is not willing to impose sanctions; as a non-member of the United Nations it maintained 'normal trade' with Rhodesia. Without a mandatory order, the sanctions net is likely to be full of holes. Japan has not adopted any strong pro-sanctions position and there could be other non-participants.

It must also be remembered that sanctions evasion through smuggling and falsification of documents was a serious problem in the Rhodesian case and there is no reason to suppose that South Africans would not be equally ingenious in their methods or their middlemen would not be equally eager to make quick profits. The record of the monitoring efforts of the Security Council Sanctions Committee between 1968 and 1979 is not encouraging.

Secondly, while South Africa is undoubtedly vulnerable to commercial and financial measures, it has formidable defences. The Rhodesian case suggests that even a weak target can sustain sanctions and if the argument is made that South Africa kept Rhodesia afloat, it must also be acknowledged that even a friendless South Africa is a much more powerful state than Rhodesia. It has an extensive coastline and very well-developed transportation systems; it is self-sufficient in food and richly endowed with minerals; it has a strong industrial base and – spurred by the UN arms embargo – manufactures and exports armaments. It has had years to build up stockpiles of oil and develop its oil from coal capacity. And it could handle some of the problems of financial sanctions by resorting to exchange control, and by relying on domestic capital.

In assessing the efficacy of UN sanctions against Rhodesia it is generally agreed that they contributed to the end of white minority rule although guerrilla warfare and the removal of Portuguese and South African support were more important. There are obvious differences between Rhodesia and South Africa, not least the numerical insignificance of the white population of Rhodesia (with the option of emigration which many took up), and its much greater vulnerability to political and economic sanctions, but there is an important similarity in that divided societies find it difficult to consolidate opposition to external pressure. The internal situation in South Africa is sufficiently disturbed to make prophecies about the future impossible; it can be predicted, however, that the defensive capabilities of the South African government, which are considerable and which would be fully deployed to offset the effects of international sanctions, would be undermined if widespread disorder becomes endemic.

Thirdly, for would-be sanctioning states, there is the question of the wider impact of comprehensive measures. As noted in Chapter 8, UN sanctions against Rhodesia had grave consequences for the economies of neighbouring states, particularly Zambia, Botswana and Mozambique. South Africa presents a more serious problem because of its dominant position in the region.

Botswana, Lesotho and Swaziland, as well as Mozambique and Zimbabwe are dependent on South Africa for their survival. There are many facets to their dependence.[31] In the first place Botswana, Lesotho, Swaziland and South Africa are members of the South African Customs Union Agreement (SACUA) established in 1910 and revised in 1969; as a result all the foreign trade of the three small states use South African ports and South Africa collects customs and import duties on their behalf. These duties account for approximately 50 per cent of their total government revenues. Secondly, South Africa provides employment for approximately 350 000 blacks from outside its borders, particularly from Lesotho, Botswana, Swaziland, Malawi and Mozambique. Most of these workers are employed on the mines and about half their earnings are remitted home each year under contractual arrangements, constituting a vital source of income for the recipient states. At least half Lesotho's Gross National Product is accounted for in this way. There are also large numbers of illegal immigrants working in South Africa; perhaps 1.2 million at any one time. South Africa has threatened to repatriate these illegal workers if employment opportunities decline sharply as a result of international sanctions, and the consequences could be very serious for neighbouring states who cannot provide alternative jobs.

Botswana, Lesotho and Swaziland are also heavily dependent on South Africa for oil, coal and electricity and for transportation services. Forty-five per cent of the external trade of Malawi, Zimbabwe, Zambia and Zaire and all the external trade of Botswana, Lesotho and Swaziland is carried by South African Transport Services rail network. Alternative routes cannot be relied upon: the Tazara railway from Zambia to Tanzania is working well below capacity and the harbour at Dar-es-Salaam is choked, while the Benguela Railway to Lobito Bay in Angola and the lines from Zimbabwe to Beira and Nacala in Mozambique are regularly put out of action by guerrilla attack. In addition to vital rail services, South Africa provides air passenger and freight services as well as service and repair facilities.

Where trade is concerned, South Africa again plays a dominant role, being the main source of exports to Botswana, Lesotho and Swaziland and an important supplier to the whole region. If these exports were seriously reduced or eliminated, the cost to the importing states of alternative supplies – even if they could be found and transported – would be much greater, placing a crippling burden on their fragile economies. Barber and Spicer are hardly overstating the case in commenting that effective sanctions against South Africa could mean that the economies of 'many of the surrounding states which are dependent on the Republic might be wrecked' while 'even partly effective sanctions ... could have their main impact in the neighbouring states'.[32] Zimbabwe, according to its Prime Minister, could not join in sanctions for these reasons.[33]

Help for these small states would place additional balance of payments burdens on western countries, who would themselves be carrying costs of sanctions. It must also be a concern that unforeseen and unwelcome effects of economic measures against South Africa could be felt in the international system as a whole through distortion of trade patterns or disturbance of financial relationships.

Finally there is the problematic connection between economic hardship inflicted on a target and its translation into political change in the required direction. Economic sanctions will be one of a number of pressures on the South African white political élite, and as already pointed out, they may accompany growing internal unrest which could involve mass strikes and/or a spread of violence into 'white' areas which have so far been relatively immune. Western governments will not want to accelerate any trend to violence or to inflict suffering on the black population of South Africa; nor do they wish to appear tolerant of repression by the South Africa government, thus alienating future black leadership. The dilemma is a very real one; there are no sanctions that can be guaranteed to produce coercive as well as punitive force; nor is there any way of ensuring either that the coercive effects will not be excessive and produce complete collapse or that the white élite will be more accommodating to reformist ideas in a worsening economic situation.

Dennis Austin suggests five steps which the South African government should be pressed to adopt; with admirable succinctness he lists them as follows: 'Politically, talk to the ANC and UDF. Socially, repeal the Group Areas Act. Economically, get rid of pass-law measures. Morally, release Nelson Mandela and his colleagues. Legally, abolish imprisonment without trial.'[34] Clear and unequivocal advocacy of these policies would give focus to western policy but what combination of measures will produce them?

In the last analysis, any peaceful solution for South Africa's problems depends on a change of heart by South African whites who have come to regard their privileged position in society as a core value which would be lost if majority rule is introduced; the alternative is violence which eventually forces whites to concede power and in the process destroys many of the achievements the Republic has to its credit and lowers the quality of life for all its inhabitants. While agreeing with Austin's policy prescriptions, one would prefer to disagree with his pessimistic conclusion that 'if revolution is averted, it will be because repression – not reform – is successful; if it is not averted, it will be because of the failure of repression'.[35] But his assessment may be realistic.

10   Sanctions Revisited

This study began with discussion of the circumstances in which international sanctions can be employed and the degree of authority which can be claimed by those imposing them and proceeded to examine a series of case studies in order to analyse the major problems associated with the sanctioning process. It is obvious that grey, not black or white, is the prevailing colour and a series of questions present themselves to the reader. To what extent are sanctions humbug? Is the sanctions label no more than a fig-leaf of respectability, available to all and fooling nobody? Are international rules inconsequential because they can be violated with impunity? What purposes do sanctions really serve?

There are no definitive answers to these questions but some general conclusions seem warranted. The first is that resort to sanctions by governments over the past decade has not accompanied or reinforced any trend towards increased authority for international institutions in dealing with international misconduct. Indeed, the reverse has been the case. The shortcomings of the United Nations are widely acknowledged and moves to reject multilateralism, particularly by the United States,[1] prompt concern about the continuing relevance of the UN and associated bodies for collective decision making in respect of rule setting and rule observance. Both authority and control are lacking.

There has certainly been progress in setting human rights standards. In particular, the group right of freedom from colonial rule has been confirmed and white minority rule has been delegitimised. These causes were taken up by the majority of UN members and ultimately were not opposed by Britain, France and other European colonial powers. Virtual consensus on mandatory UN sanctions was possible for Rhodesia which violated these norms and was technically a British self-governing colony to which Britain could dictate terms for independence assuring majority rule. South Africa, although a sovereign state, now stands universally condemned for its system of apartheid and for its retention of Namibia and there is a growing body of opinion favouring sanctions against it. As we have seen, the arms trade with South Africa was designated a threat to the peace and banned by the Security Council in 1977: by July 1985 the Council was prepared to encourage UN members to impose voluntary economic sanctions.

But these are isolated instances concerning a particular set of issues. It is true that in certain other cases where UN members have clearly violated international standards of behaviour the Security Council has condemned them, although it has not taken the additional step of recommending or ordering sanctions. Iran, Argentina and Israel have been censured in this way. But more often than not, whether human rights violations, resort to force or the breach of other international obligations are involved, the Security Council takes no disciplinary action at all. The General Assembly has also been selectively critical: condemnation and recommendations for sanctions coming from that body have not usually been directed at Third World governments even when – as in the case of the Amin regime in Uganda – they were clearly merited.

A major flaw in designs for international enforcement through the League of Nations and the UN was the assumption that governments would be prepared to censure and punish international wrong-doing at the expense of their own interests. As they are not prepared to do so, sanctions do not generally enjoy firm status as measures supporting community norms and they lack deterrent power. In fact, as we have seen, there is often no agreement that wrong-doing has occurred and the pattern of response is therefore highly erratic. Typically the key factor is not the nature of state conduct but the status of the rule-breaker (be it a permanent member of the Security Council or a non-aligned Third World state) and its relationship to other governments.

One can ask whether compliance with group norms as a result of sanctions is more likely to be sought or achieved in limited-member organisations. Such bodies may be regionally based, like the Organisation of American States and the Organisation of African Unity, or linked by other bonds, such as the historic ties between Commonwealth countries or the shared faith of members of the Islamic Conference. Values and norms can be affirmed in such settings and where one member 'deviates', disapproval of its conduct, expressed through sanctions, can have credibility as a collective expression of support for these values. The censure of the Council of Europe for the excesses of the Greek junta and the forced withdrawal of South Africa from the Commonwealth are cases in point. But as at the UN, there may be no consensus on the 'rules' or on the need for sanctions, either because the grounds for imposing them are disputed within the organisation, or because political considerations dictate inaction.

In organisations dominated by a hegemonic power the likelihood of sanctions may be greater. Such powers can exert a strong influence in setting and interpreting rules, as well as in enforcing them. In the 1960s the United States was able to work through the OAS to isolate and discipline Cuba; the USSR has used the Warsaw Pact to crush moves for autonomy in Eastern Europe. These regional actions are not particularly reassuring models for international sanctions. Experience over the past decade suggests however that the current trend is for sanctions to be imposed outside organisational frameworks and this makes the picture even more blurred: there is no basis for predicting sanctions in relation to acts of wrong-doing and no prior commitment to respond. Salience of interest to states considering the imposition of sanctions and calculations of advantage and disadvantage prompt *ad hoc* decisions on whether to respond or not in each case. Unilateralism is an inevitable outcome.

The second broad conclusion is that any assessment of the efficacy of sanctions must be linked to their purposes, whether or not these purposes are publicly expressed. As noted in Chapter 6, sanctions may be designed as expressions of disapproval rather than as punitive or coercive measures; it is also possible that their rationale may be found in image politics: the desire to show sensitivity to moral issues, strength in the face of threats to national security, leadership in combating undesirable trends. Alternatively, pressure may emanate from the domestic population of the governments instigating them or from third states. It is true that collective economic measures have not generally proved a reliable means of bringing compliance from their targets, but if sanctions are merely symbolic, or are principally designed to satisfy domestic opinion or to meet an ally's expectations of 'solidarity', then economic impact on the target is not crucial, and may not even be particularly important.

Thirdly, both ethical and prudential considerations are relevant to the imposition of economic sanctions which *are* intended to have a significant impact. Wreaking economic havoc on an impoverished developing country which is aleady unable to meet the basic needs of its people hardly commends itself as appropriate action, even if the foreign or domestic policy of the country concerned merits an international response. And even in countries like Poland and South Africa the question of where the burden of sacrifice will actually fall needs to be considered. The Rhodesian government shifted the main weight of economic hardship on to the black population and protected whites. Resulting unemployment may have helped recruitment for the guerrilla forces of the Patriotic Front but presumably that was not the intention of the sanctioning powers.

Ethical considerations are also relevant in considering the spillover effects of sanctions which could be serious or even disastrous for innocent neighbouring states. The implications of sanctions for South Africa's neighbours were explored in the previous chapter. And prudence dictates a concern for unwanted and perhaps uncontrollable systemic consequences of economic measures: provoking debt default or undermining confidence in the international financial system are two examples of possible systemic effects which recent cases have highlighted.

The case studies examined in this book suggest that a serious problem with sanctioning in the international milieu is the impossibility in most cases of applying discrete penalties to discrete acts of illegal or unacceptable conduct. Neither 'act' nor 'response' can be effectively separated from the general flow of accompanying and ensuing events. Even when the 'act' is reasonably clear cut, as with Argentina's seizure of the Falkland Islands, or the shooting down of KAL Flight 007, responses become part of the outcome and have a bearing on future developments. And where would-be sanctionists confront an ongoing situation, such as South Africa's apartheid policies or the existence of repressive regimes in the Soviet Union and Poland, there is much greater difficulty in making penalties credible. One might argue that sanctions are best seen as a contribution to the solution of a problem: influential, if not decisive. But what if they become part of a new set of problems, making peaceful resolution more, not less difficult? As political signals they may be misinterpreted; by initiating a chain reaction they may do great harm. And will it be possible to terminate them if they become obviously counterproductive, without giving the wrong message both to the target and to other audiences?

Doubtless, governments will continue to grapple with the problems of sanctions, while scholars analyse and compare cases where they have been – or may be – used. Three general comments seem to be worth making, all of which have policy implications. The first returns to the question of costs and specifically cost-effectiveness. As non-lethal measures economic sanctions are generally preferable to the use of force and send stronger signals than diplomatic and political measures. David Baldwin has pointed out that 'policy alternatives with clearly discernible higher utility' are not always 'easy to identify'.[2] But if the economic cost of economic measures to their instigator(s) exceeds their economic cost to the target, there should surely be compensating political benefits for the former and/or additional political costs for the latter. The United States grain embargo in 1980–1 is estimated to have been at least as costly for the American as for the Soviet economy; the political costs of the pipeline embargo in terms of serious intra-alliance strains were obvious. Were there compensating political benefits for the United States in these cases? And if it is unsatisfactory for the major cost of sanctions to be carried by those imposing them, it is also undesirable to launch measures which place undue burdens on third parties or produce disproportionately damaging systemic effects. Discounting the probable economic impact of economic sanctions on targets would seem nowadays to be fairly common but it is by no means clear that the need for careful forecasting of all relevant costs is fully understood.[3]

The second consideration for policy makers is not only that sanctions may be ineffectual in modifying the target's behaviour where this is seriously sought, but that they could produce the opposite effects from those intended; in particular, the target may be driven to adopt defiant and perhaps more extreme positions as a result of sanctions. Rhodesia resisted British, Commonwealth and UN pressure and became more dependent on South Africa; Cuba was forced to move into a close alliance with the Soviet Union; West European governments fear that Nicaragua will be driven into the arms of Cuba and the Soviet Union; Arab support for Libya seemed to be enhanced rather than diminished by US sanctions. Exclusion from international organisations may also be counterproductive by eliminating opportunities for dialogue and diplomacy.

Because of the danger of solidifying rather than modifying the target's behaviour, Richard Olson has suggested that subtle measures are politically more effective even if their economic effects are moderate; 'high-profile sanctions must be avoided if compliance is the goal'.[4] Similar considerations prompted Samuel Huntington to advocate rewards and punishments as the best form of leverage.[5] But collective international sanctions of the kind we have been concerned with in this study can hardly be covert. A combination of sticks and carrots may be more promising for problem solving but it will obviously present serious policy dilemmas and co-ordination difficulties for groups of states, particularly if they are operating in an *ad hoc* coalition.

The third issue concerns the current and future status of international sanctions. Lack of consensus at the United Nations has produced decentralised and fragmented sanctioning, where one or more states act independently as guardians and enforcers of acceptable behaviour. The Soviet Union has adopted this role in Eastern Europe and the United States is displaying a growing propensity to act in a 'disciplinary' capacity on a global scale. Perhaps inevitably, such roles are exercised with selectivity: Iran, the Soviet Union, Poland, Nicaragua and Libya have been subjected to US sanctions, but until recently there was great reluctance to impose measures on South Africa and Israel has been protected rather than reproved. Meanwhile, the twelve members of the European Community who form an important political and economic grouping, have preferred to distance themselves from US-sponsored sanctions, challenging the need or justification for them and expressing scepticism about their efficacy.

There is an obvious danger that 'sanctions' will lose their status as measures which genuinely support universally-accepted standards of behaviour, and be seen increasingly as nothing more than labels for politically-motivated action taken by governments in their own interests. Given the real progress which has been made since the Second World War in developing rules which limit both the use of force and the abuse of human rights, this would be a retrograde development. Western countries, including the United States, should consider carefully the long-term advantages of adopting an even-handed and consistent pattern of response to acts of foreign aggression, gross and persistent violations of human rights and, perhaps, proven sponsorship of international terrorist acts against innocent people. Collective resort to the UN as the forum of first resort to condemn such acts, and to associate other states with such condemnation, would send clear signals to wrong-doers and provide the opportunity to use the UN's authority to the greatest extent possible. Britain's initial use of the UN in the Falklands crisis was an appropriate procedure. If an adequate response cannot be organised within the UN framework, it would also be preferable if sanctions to be imposed by Western governments were agreed upon prior to their announcement, thus maximising symbolic impact as well as limiting the damage to the West which is inflicted by open quarrelling. The likelihood that any agreed set of measures would be mild rather than severe is not necessarily a drawback; harsh measures which are not widely supported will be less efficacious and may also have the counterproductive effects discussed above. In fact, measures chosen from the mild end of the sanctions spectrum offer several advantages: the possibility of unanimity; the option of moving to severer measures at a later stage; and scope for the simultaneous pursuit of negotiated solutions to the problem at hand. The policies adopted by the United States, the European Community and the Commonwealth in the autumn of 1985, which combined a set of mild sanctions and the threat of further penalties with a serious attempt to use diplomatic pressure to bring an end to apartheid in South Africa, appeared to offer an encouraging model for concerted action of a similar kind in other situations. Where sanctions clearly support community interests, the effort to produce consistent and co-ordinated policies is well worth making.

Notes and References

1 The Scope of the Study

1. See D. A. Baldwin, *Economic Statecraft* (Princeton, New Jersey: Princeton University Press, 1985); M. S. Daoudi and M. S. Dajani, *Economic Sanctions: Ideals and Experience* (London: Routledge & Kegan Paul, 1983); M. P. Doxey, *Economic Sanctions and International Enforcement*, 2nd edn (London: Macmillan for the Royal Institute of International Affairs, 1980); G. C. Hufbauer and J. J. Schott, *Economic Sanctions Reconsidered: History and Current Policy* (Washington, DC: Institute for International Economics, 1985); D. L. Losman, *International Economic Sanctions: the cases of Cuba, Israel and Rhodesia* (Albuquerque, New Mexico: University of New Mexico Press, 1979); R. Renwick, *Economic Sanctions* (London: Croom Helm, 1982). See too J. Barber, Economic Sanctions as a Policy Instrument', *International Affairs*, vol. 55, 3 (1979) 367–84; R. S. Olson, 'Economic Coercion in World Politics with a Focus on North–South Relations', *World Politics*, vol.. 31, 4 (1979) 471–94.
2. *Economic Statecraft*, 35–6.
3. Ibid., 30.
4. See J. Galtung, 'On the Effects of International Economic Sanctions with examples from the case of Rhodesia', *World Politics*, vol. 19, 3 (1967) 378–416.
5. See D. A. Baldwin, 'The Power of Positive Sanctions', *World Politics*, vol. 24, 1 (1971) 19–38.
6. *Economic Statecraft*, 36.
7. R. S. Olson suggests that 'coercion' should be interchangeable with 'sanction' in meaning. Loc. cit. in n. 1 above, 472–4.
8. *Economic Statecrat*, 36.
9. Ibid.
10. See D. W. Bowett, 'Economic Coercion and Reprisals by States', *The Virginia Journal of International Law*, vol. 13, 1 (1972) 1–12.
11. Klaus Knorr lists seven typical goals in pursuit of which governments use economic power; only one – 'symbolizing displeasure and inflicting punishment' – is relevant to sanctions. *Power and Wealth: The Political Economy of International Power* (New York: Basic Books, 1973) ch. 6. See too O. R. Young, *Compliance and Public Authority: A Theory with International Applications* (Baltimore, Maryland: Johns Hopkins University Press, 1980) 35.

12. On Arab boycotts see C. C. Joyner, 'The Transnational Boycott as Economic Coercion in International Law: Policy, Place and Practice. *Vanderbilt Journal of Transnational Law*, vol. 17, 2 (1984) 205–86; N. Turck, 'The Arab Boycott of Israel', *Foreign Affairs*, vol. 55, 3 (1977) 472–93.

13. Bowett loc. cit. in n. 10, 9.

14. See Judith Miller 'When Sanctions Worked', *Foreign Policy*, no. 39 (Summer 1980) 118–29; R. H. Ullman 'Human Rights and Economic Power: the US vs. Idi Amin', *Foreign Affairs*, vol. 56, 3 (1979) 529–43; S. J. Fredman, 'US Trade Sanctions against Uganda', *Law and Policy in International Business*, vol. 11, 3 (1979) 1149–61.

15. See Hedley Bull (ed.), *Intervention in World Politics* (London: Oxford University Press, 1984); Michael Walzer, *Just and Unjust Wars* (New York: Basic Books, 1977); Jack Donnelly, 'Human Rights, Humanitarian Intervention and American Foreign Policy', *Journal of International Affairs*, vol. 37, 2 (1984) 311–28.

16. See *US Department of State Memorandum: Legal Basis for the Quarantine of Cuba* (Washington, DC 23 October 1962).

17. See R. B. Lillich, 'Economic Coercion and the International Legal Order', *International Affairs*, vol. 51, 3 (1975) 358–71.

18. See GATT, CN 159, 10 August 1982.

19. For instance a consumer boycott of Nestlé products co-ordinated by the Infant Formula Action Committee (INFACT) was instrumental in persuading the company to bring its advertising and marketing procedures for infant formula into line with the World Health Organisation code. See T. Lemaresquier, 'Beyond Infant Feeding ...' *Development Dialogue*, 1980:1, 120–5.

2   International Standards and the Authoritative Basis for Sanctions

1. Neither the Covenant nor the Charter uses the word 'sanction' but the enforcement measures envisaged in both documents have always been so described. D. Mitrany wrote in 1925 that 'the term ... sanctions has now passed into general usage for describing collectively the various means prescribed or contemplated for enforcing international covenants'. *The Problem of International Sanctions* (London: Oxford University Press, 1925). 1

2. As noted in Chapter 1, military measures cannot be ordered because agreements to make forces available under Article 43 have never been concluded.

3. Cf. Sir Anton Bertram's comment that 'the economic weapon, conceived not as an instrument of war but as a means of peaceful

pressure, is the great discovery and the most precious possession of the League'. 'The Economic Weapon as a Form of Peaceful Pressure', 17 *Transactions of the Grotius Society* (1932) 141.

4. Article 2 (7) of the Charter confirms the exclusiveness of domestic jurisdiction but states that 'this principle shall not prejudice the application of enforcement measures under Chapter VII'.

5. Ian Clark, *Reform and Resistance in the International Order* (London: Cambridge University Press, 1980) ch. 5, especially 18–19.

6. Ibid.

7. G. W. Baer, 'Sanctions and Security: the League of Nations and the Italo-Ethiopian War, 1935–1936', *International Organization*, vol. 27, 2 (1973) 166.

8. S. S. Kim, *The Quest for a Just World Order* (Boulder, Colorado: Westview Press, 1984) Table 6.1, 217.

9. See further discussion in Chapter 6.

10. See M. Reisman 'The Legal Effect of Vetoed Resolutions', *American Journal of International Law*, vol. 74, 4 (1980) 904–7.

11. Ibid., 906. See too Oscar Schachter's comment that a draft resolution 'that is not adopted should have neither affirmative nor negative legal consequences', 'Self-help in International Law', *Journal of International Affairs*, vol. 37, 2 (1984) 238.

12. D. W. Bowett 'Economic Coercion and Reprisals by States', *The Virginia Journal of International Law*, vol. 13, 1 (1972) 6 and n. 23.

13. For a review of opinions on the legal significance of Assembly resolutions see C. C. Joyner 'UN General Assembly Resolutions and International Law: Rethinking the Contemporary Dynamics of Norm Creation', *California Western International Law Journal*, vol. 11, 3 (1981) 445–78.

14. The International Monetary Fund and the World Bank are required by their Articles of Agreement to remain above politics but in practice all UN agencies reflect political influence and the political will of member states.

15. See Joseph Gold, 'The "sanctions" of the International Monetary Fund', *American Journal of International Law*, vol. 66, 5 (1972) 737–62 and 'Strengthening the Soft International Law of Exchange Arrangements', ibid., vol. 77, 3 (1983) 443–89.

16. See R. E. Bissell, *Apartheid and International Organizations* (Boulder, Colorado: Westview Press, 1977). For comments on the generally unsuccessful effort by Third World countries to subject Israel to the same treatment as South Africa see E. Gross, 'On the Degradation of the Constitutional Environment of the United Nations', *American Journal of International Law*, vol. 77, 3 (1983) 569–88.

17. Politically the US made it clear as early as 1954 in connection with Guatemala that the Security Council would not be permitted

to challenge US hegemony in the Western hemisphere. See *UN Security Council Official Records*, 676th meeting, 25 June 1954, para. 168.

18. A majority vote of the Committee of Ministers was anticipated, suspending Greece from membership until democratic freedoms were restored as required by Article 3 of the Statute. The European Commission on Human Rights had presented a well-documented account of the suppression of human rights and fundamental freedoms to the Committee. See *The Greek Case: Report of the European Commission on Human Rights* (in 4 volumes), 18 November 1969.

19. The Brezhnev Doctrine is discussed further in Chapter 5.

20. T. Nardin, *Law, Morality and the Relations of States* (Princeton, New Jersey: Princeton University Press, 1983), particularly 133–48.

21. Ibid., 111.

22. Bowett, loc. cit. in n. 12 above, 9.

23. See Jack Donnelly 'Human Rights, Humanitarian Intervention and American Foreign Policy: Law, Morality and Politics', *Journal of International Affairs*, 37, 2 (1984) 320.

3   League of Nations Sanctions

1. The vote for military measures was over 6.75 million. See F. P. Walters, *A History of the League of Nations*, vol. II (London: Oxford University Press for the Royal Institute of International Affairs, 1952) 636, 706.

2. Details in *Dispute Between Ethiopia and Italy*, Cmd. 5071 (London: HMSO, 1936) 43–50.

3. Frank Hardie, *The Abyssinian Crisis* (London: Batsford, 1974) 102.

4. See *Dispute Between Italy and Ethiopia*, Cmd.. 5094 (London: HMSO, 1936).

5. Lord Avon's comments are in *The Eden Memoirs: Facing the Dictators* (London: Cassell, 1962) 384–5. See too Hardie, *Abyssinian Crisis*, 223–4.

6. See *The Economist*, 6 June 1936, 542.

7. H. V. Hodson in A. J. Toynbee, *Survey of International Affairs 1935*, vol. II (London: Oxford University Press for the Royal Institute of International Affairs, 1936) 435.

8. *The Economist*, 12 October 1935, 694.

9. R. Renwick, *Economic Sanctions* (London: Croom Helm, 1982) 22.

10. Mussolini is reported to have said in 1938 that if League sanctions had included oil, he would have had to withdraw from Ethiopia 'within a week'. P. Schmidt, *Hitler's Interpreter*, ed. R. H. C. Steed (New York: Macmillan, 1951) 60.

11. See .W. A. Riddell, ed., *Documents on Canadian Foreign Policy 1917–1939* (Toronto: Oxford University Press, 1962), 575.
12. See F. P. Walters, *A History of the League of Nations* (London: Oxford University Press, 1960) 771–3.

4 United Nations Sanctions

1. G. A. Resolution 3379, 10 November 1975. Withholding of the United States dues to UNESCO in 1974 and to the IAEA in 1982 brought reinstatement of Israel to full participation in both these agencies; in 1975 the US Senate resolved that if Israel were expelled from the UN the Senate would review US aid to states supporting the expulsion and would consider seriously the implications of continued membership for the United States in the UN itself. See E. Gross 'On the Degradation of the Constitutional Environment of the United Nations', *American Journal of International Law*, 77, 3 (1983) 569–88.
2. See Elaine Windrich, *Britain and the Politics of Rhodesian Independence* (London: Croom Helm, 1978); R. C. Good, *UDI: The International Politics of the Rhodesian Rebellion* (London: Faber, 1973).
3. See *Rhodesia: Documents Relating to Proposals for a Settlement 1966*, Cmnd. 3171 (London: HMSO, 1966) 3.
4. House of Commons *Debates*, 1 November 1965, vol. 718, coll. 633 f.
5. Commonwealth Prime Ministers' Meeting in Lagos 1966: *Final Communique*, Cmnd. 2890 (London: HMSO, 1966) 5.
6. *Rhodesia: Report of the [Pearce] Commission on Rhodesian Opinion*, Cmnd. 4964 (London: HMSO, 1972). The Pearce Commission reported that: 'Mistrust of the intentions and motives of the [Rhodesian] government transcended all other considerations', 80.
7. The ups and downs of Rhodesian–South African relations are well-chronicled in H. R. Strack, *Sanctions: The Case of Rhodesia* (Syracuse, New York: Syracuse University Press, 1978).
8. There was also a demand from the US Congress that President Carter should terminate sanctions unless he determined it to be in the national interest not to do so. He did so determine.
9. See *Southern Rhodesia: Report of the Constitutional Conference, Lancaster House, London, Sept.–Dec. 1979*, Cmnd. 7802 (London: HMSO, 1980). See also Lord Soames 'From Rhodesia to Zimbabwe', *International Affairs*, vol. 56, 3 (1980) 405–19.
10. See *Tenth Report* of the UN Sanctions Committee, S/12529 rev. 1., vol. II, 5.
11. D. G. Clarke comments that 'the regime in large measure subordinated domestic policy to balance of payments considerations'.

'Zimbabwe's International Economic Position and aspects of sanctions removal', *Journal of Commonwealth and Comparative Politics*, 18, 1 (1980) 38. Details of NCI (no currency involved) deals are in Strack, *Sanctions*, in n. 7, 106–7.

12. M. Bailey and B. Rivers, *Oil Sanctions Against Rhodesia* (London: Commonwealth Secretariat, 1977).

13. T. Bingham and S. M. Gray, *Report on the Supply of Petroleum and Petroleum Products to Rhodesia* (London: Foreign and Commonwealth Office, HMSO, 1978). See too Brian White 'Britain and the Implementation of Oil Sanctions against Rhodesia' in Steve Smith and Michael Clarke (eds) *Foreign Policy Implementation* (London: George Allen and Unwin, 1985).

14. The Bingham Report, 216.

15. See Strack, *Sanctions: the Case of Rhodesia* and Renwick *Economic Sanctions* for thoughtful, informed comments. D. G. Clarke gives an economist's analysis in 'Zimbabwe's International Economic Position and aspects of sanctions removal', loc. cit. in n. 11 above.

16. Cited in Renwick, Table VIII, 101.

17. South West Africa Cases (Second Phase) ICJ *Reports*, 1966, 6.

18. Legal Consequences for States of the Continued Presence of South Africa in Namibia (South West Africa) notwithstanding Security Council Resolution 276 (1970), ICJ *Reports* 1971, 16.

19. US Executive Order of 9 September 1985 in *International Legal Materials*, XXIV, 5 (September 1985) 1488–90. The Sullivan code, proposed by Rev. Leon Sullivan, a black Baptist minister in Philadelphia, sets out principles of non-discriminatory hiring and promotion practices which should be observed by subsidiaries of US companies in South Africa. The EC has adopted a more stringent code; see n. 22 below.

20. US Department of State *Bulletin* 1491, 9 September 1985.

21. See report of Ministerial Meeting on Political Co-operation, *International Legal Materials* XXIV, 5 (September 1985) 1479–84.

22. *The Code of Conduct for EEC Companies with subsidiaries, branches or representation in South Africa* was adopted on 20 September 1977. See Brussels: Commission of the European Communities, *Information*, 'The EEC in Southern Africa', 166/77 E, Annex.

23. For instance Mrs Thatcher is on record as saying that 'there is no earthly use in creating unemployment at home in order to create unemployment there [in South Africa] which is why I am against sanctions and still am against sanctions, added to which they won't work' (Pretoria: *South African Digest*, 25 October 1985) 971.

24. *The Commonwealth Accord on Southern Africa*, 20 October 1985 (London: Commonwealth Secretariat News Release 85/28, 22 October 1985) 1.

25. Ibid., 2–3.
26. Ibid. Mrs Thatcher made it clear that her government would not support these additional measures.

5 Sanctions in Regional Settings

1. Comecon deals specifically with economic co-ordination and planning and has non-European as well as European members. Cuba, Vietnam and Mongolia are full members; others, e.g. Nicaragua, send observers to meetings.
2. 'Economic Sanctions as a Policy Instrument', *International Affairs*, vol. 55, 3 (1979) 371. Emphasis added.
3. A full account of measures against Yugoslavia is in *White Book on Aggressive Activities by the Government of the USSR ... towards Yugoslavia* (Belgrade: Ministry of Foreign Affairs, 1951). Romania even cut rail and postal links with Yugoslavia in 1950.
4. See R. B. Farrell, *Yugoslavia and the Soviet Union 1948–1956: An Analysis with Documents* (Hamden, Connecticut: Shoestring Press, 1956); *UN Economic Survey of Europe in 1953* (Geneva, 1954) 111–12; R. O. Freedman, *Economic Warfare in the Soviet Bloc: a study of Soviet Economic Pressure against Yugoslavia, Albania and Communist China* (New York: Praeger, 1970).
5. See S. C. Stolte 'Albania under Economic Pressure from Moscow', *Bulletin* (Munich), vol. 9, 3 (1962) 25–34; Freedman, loc. cit. in n. 4.
6. The Brezhnev Doctrine was formulated in a *Pravda* Commentary by S. Kovalyov on 26 September 1968 entitled 'Sovereignty and International Obligations of Socialist Countries', and reiterated by the Soviet Foreign Minister at the UN on 3 October and by Brezhnev at the 5th Congress of the Polish Communist Party on 12 November.
7. T. M Franck and E. Weisband, *Word Politics: Verbal Strategy Among the Superpowers* (New York: Oxford University Press, 1972).
8. See Chapter 1, n. 16.
9. The General Assembly condemned the US action as a 'flagrant violation of international law' by a vote of 108 : 9 with 27 abstentions, res. 38/7 (xxxviii), 2 November 1983. For differing scholarly perspectives on the US intervention in Grenada see the *American Journal of International Law*, vol. 78, 1 (1984) 131–75; see too W. C. Gilmore, *The Grenada Intervention: analysis and documentation* (London: Mansell Publishing Limited, 1984).
10. The US contested the Court's jurisdiction and withdrew from the case in January 1985 after the Court ruled that it in fact had jurisdiction and gave an interim judgement that the US should stop supporting military activity aimed at the overthrow of the

Nicaraguan government. See Military and Paramilitary Activities in and against Nicaragua (Nicaragua v. United States) Jurisdiction and Admissability, ICJ *Reports*, 1984, 392. In February 1985 President Reagan acknowledged that the US was seeking to overthrow the Sandinista government, *New York Times*, 22 February 1985, A10, cols. 1, 3.

11. *UN Yearbook of International Trade Statistics 1963* (New York: 1965) 210–11.
12. Anna P. Schreiber 'Economic Coercion as an Instrument of Foreign Policy: US Economic Measures against Cuba and the Dominican Republic', *World Politics*, vol. 25, 3 (1973) 409.
13. See R. St. J. Macdonald, 'The Organization of American States in Action', *University of Toronto Law Journal*, vol. 15 (1964) 325–429; Jerome Slater, *Intervention and Negotiation: the United States and the Dominican Republic* (London: Harper, 1970).
14. Eighth Meeting of Ministers of Foreign Affairs of the Organisation of American States, Punta del Este, January 1962, *Final Act* (Washington DC: Pan American Union) OEA/Ser. C/II.8.
15. See A. Chayes, The Cuban Missile Crisis: *International Crisis and the Role of Law* (London: Oxford University Press, 1974).
16. See M. H. Morley, 'The United States and the Global Economic Blockade of Cuba: A Study in Political Pressures on America's Allies', *Canadian Journal of Political Science*, vol. 17, 1 (1984) 25–48.
17. Schreiber, "Economic Coercion', 395.
18. See *UN Yearbook of International Trade Statistics* 1960 (New York 1962), 154.
19. Schreiber, 'Economic Coercion', 389.
20. See Jorge I. Dominguez, 'Cuba in the 1980s', *Problems of Communism*, vol. 30 (March–April 1981) 50.
21. See A. R. M. Ritter, *The Economic Development of Revolutionary Cuba: Strategy and Performance* (New York: Praeger, 1974) 96.
22. Ibid., 209.
23. See, for instance, Jorge I. Dominguez, *Cuba: Order and Revolution* (Cambridge, Massachusetts: Harvard University Press, 1978).
24. Ritter notes that 'for the latter years of the 1960s, the journalistic estimate of $1 million per day [from the USSR] is probably an underestimate', *Economic Development of Revolutionary Cuba*, 210.
25. Official aims in 1964 as set out by Under-Secretary of State George Ball were to reduce the will and ability of the Cuban regime to export subversion and violence; to make it plain to the Cuban people that the Castro regime could not serve their interests; to demonstrate to the people of the Western hemisphere that communism had no future there and to increase costs to the USSR of maintaining an 'outpost' as noted. See US Department of State,

American Foreign Policy: Current Documents 1964 (Washington, DC: 1967) 323, 324.

26. R. Blackburn in E. de Kadt (ed.) *Patterns of Foreign Influence in the Caribbean* (London: Oxford University Press for the Royal Institute of International Affairs, 1972) 139.

27. For conflicting perspectives on the legality of the Arab oil embargoes of 1973–4 see J. J. Paust and A. P. Blaustein, 'The Arab Oil Weapon: A Threat to International Peace', *American Journal of International Law*, vol. 68, 3 (1974) 410–39; I. Shihata, 'Destination Embargo of Arab Oil: Its Legality under International Law', ibid., vol. 68, 4 (1974) 591–627.

28. See, for instance, *Israeli Settlements in the Occupied Territories.* Hearings before the Subcommittees on International Organisations and Europe and the Middle East of the House of Representatives Committee on International Relations, 95th Congress, 1st session. 12, 21 September and 19 October 1977 (Washington, DC: US GPO, 1978).

29. See Victor Lavy, 'The Economic Embargo of Egypt by Arab States: Myth and Reality', *The Middle East Journal*, vol. 38, 3 (1984) 425.

30. See, for instance, the report in the *Daily Telegraph*, 10 July 1979.

31. Lavy, 'Economic Embargo of Egypt', 427.

32. See G. C. Hufbauer and J. J. Schott, *Economic Sanctions Reconsidered*, 610.

33. Keesing's *Contemporary Archives*, 1979, 29953B.

6 Sanctions outside Organisational Frameworks

1. Iran's claims are reproduced in the Court's Order of 15 December 1979 (1979 ICJ *Reports*, 10–11) and its judgement of 24 May 1980 (1980 ICJ *Reports*, 8–9).

2. Customary law on this subject was codified in the Vienna Conventions on Diplomatic Relations (1961) and on Consular Relations (1963).

3. 1979 ICJ *Reports*, 10–11.

4. East Germany also voted 'no'; Mexico and Bangladesh abstained; China did not participate.

5. Diplomatic relations were severed on 4 April 1980.

6. O. Schachter, 'Self-help in International Law', *Journal of International Affairs*, vol. 37, 2 (1984) 232.

7. 1980 ICJ *Reports*, 43. For a strong indictment of many aspects of US policy in this crisis see F. A. Boyle, *World Politics and International Law* (Durham, North Carolina: Duke University Press, 1985).

8. See Keesing's *Contemporary Archives*, 1981, 31083.
9. See report in *The Times*, 15 December 1979.
10. 'Economic Sanctions and the Iran Experience', *Foreign Affairs*, vol. 60, 2 (1981–2) 247–65.
11. Ibid., 254.
12. Opposing views on the threat posed by Soviet intervention are set out in *NATO after Afghanistan*: a report prepared for the US House of Representatives Committee on Foreign Affairs (Washington, DC: USGPO, 27 October 1980).
13. See report in the *Daily Telegraph*, 17 June 1981.
14. *Manchester Guardian Weekly*, 8 June 1980.
15. J. Hajda, 'The Soviet Grain Embargo', *Survival*, November–December 1980, 255. See too John C. Roney, 'Grain Embargo as a Diplomatic Lever: a case study of the US–Soviet Grain Embargo of 1980–1' in US Congress Joint Economic Committee, *The Soviet Economy in the 1980s*, Part II (Washington, DC: 97th Congress, 2nd session 1982).
16. See the discussion in Chapter 7 below. J. P. Hardt and Kate Tomlinson comment that the embargo was 'a poor third as a causal factor' in the shortfall of Soviet meat production, behind bad weather and systemic problems. See Abraham S. Becker (ed.) *Economic Relations with the USSR* (Lexington, Massachusetts: D. C. Heath, 1983) ch. 5, 90.
17. See G. Adler-Karlsson, *Western Economic Warfare 1947–1967; a Case Study in Foreign Economic Policy* (Stockholm: Almqvist and Wiksell, 1968); A. S. Becker (ed.) *Economic Relations with the USSR*, app. 5A: 'COCOM's operating procedures ...'
18. D. A. Baldwin, *Economic Statecraft*, 214–24.
19. See statement by W. A. Wallis, Under-Secretary for Economic Affairs, Department of State, in *East–West Economic Issues, Sanctions Policy, and the Formulation of International Economic Policy*. Hearings before subcommittees of the House of Representatives Committee on Foreign Affairs, 98th Congress, Second Session, 29 March 1984 (Washington, DC: USGPO, 1984) 4.
20. Regulations were promulgated under the US Export Administration Act 1979.
21. See Department of External Affairs (Ottawa) *Communique*, no. 121, 9 August 1982.
22. See report in the *New York Times*, 23 July 1982.
23. See the *Financial Times*, 27 August 1982.
24. A thoughtful discussion can be found in Schachter loc. cit. in n. 6 above, 238–41.
25. See statement by W. A. Wallis cited in n. 19 above.
26. See A. P. Rubin, 'Historical and Legal Background of the Falk-

land/Malvinas Dispute' in A. R. Coll and A. C. Arend (eds) *The Falklands War: lessons for strategy, diplomacy and international law* (London: Allen and Unwin, 1985) 9–21; F. S. Northedge, 'The Falkland Islands: Origins of the British Involvement', *International Relations*, vol. 7, 4 (1982) 2167–89.

27. See (Sir) Anthony Parsons, 'The Falklands Crisis in the United Nations', *International Affairs*, vol. 59, 2 (1983) 169–78.

28. J. Norton Moore deplores the 'tilt from fundamental charter principles to a supposed overriding regionalism' reflected in this resolution. 'The Inter-American System snarls in Falklands War', *American Journal of International Law*, vol. 76, 4 (1982) 831.

29. See *The Times*, 10 July and 13 July 1982.

30. P. Calvert, *The Falklands Crisis: the Rights and the Wrongs* (London: Frances Pinter, 1982) 124.

31. A report in the *Manchester Guardian Weekly* of 14 June 1985 noted that Scotch whisky was included under this heading.

32. See, for instance, T. M. Franck, 'Dulce et Decorum Est: the Strategic Role of Legal Principle in the Falklands War', *American Journal of International Law*, vol. 77, 1 (1983) 109–24.

7 Problems for States Applying Sanctions

1. This useful distinction is made by A. C. Lamborn in 'Risk and Foreign Policy Choice', *International Studies Quarterly*, vol. 29, 4 (December 1985) 385–410.

2. See David A. Baldwin, *Economic Statecraft* (Princeton: New Jersey: Princeton University Press, 1985) 243, 281–2; *NATO after Afghanistan*: a report prepared for the US House of Representatives Committee on Foreign Affairs, USGPO, (Washington, DC, 27 October 1980).

3. Barber distinguished between primary, secondary and tertiary objectives. See 'Economic Sanctions as a Policy Instrument', *International Affairs*, vol. 55, 3 (1979) 367–84.

4. On Cuba see US Department of State, *American Foreign Policy, Current Documents 1964* (1967) 323–4; on Afghanistan, US Department of State, *Current Policy*, No. 194 (Washington, DC: 5 June 1980).

5. *Economic Statecraft*, 261–7.

6. Ibid., 264.

7. See M. Doxey, 'Strategies in Multilateral Diplomacy: The Commonwealth, Southern Africa and the NIEO', *International Journal*, vol. 35, 2 (Spring 1980) 329–56.

8. For instance in the Tehran hostages crisis, the Minister of State at the Foreign and Commonwealth Office stated in evidence to

the Parliamentary Foreign Affairs Committee that the alternative
to imposing economic sanctions on Iran was not to do nothing
but 'to go back to the President of the United States and slap him
in the face'. *Afghanistan: the Soviet Invasion and the Consequences for
British Policy*, 5th Report of the Foreign Affairs Committee, UK
House of Commons Paper No. 745 (30 July 1980) 194. See too
M. Mastanduno, 'Strategies of Economic Containment: US trade
relations with the Soviet Union', *World Politics*, vol. 37, 4 (July
1985) 521.

9. *New York Times*, 16 November 1982. The French government
denied that any agreement had been reached.
10. The standard work on East–West trade controls is G. Adler-
Karlsson, *Western Economic Warfare 1947–1967: a case-study in foreign
economic policy* (Stockholm: Almqvist and Wiksell, 1968). See too
J. R. McIntyre and R. T. Cupitt 'East–West Strategic Trade
Controls: crumbling consensus', *Survey*, vol. 25 (1980) 81–108.
11. H. Strack, *Sanctions: the Case of Rhodesia* (Syracuse, New York:
Syracuse University Press, 1978) 132–4.
12. Cf. J. Galtung, 'On the Effects of International Economic Sanctions with examples from the case of Rhodesia', *World Politics*,
vol. 19, 3 (April 1967) 378–416.
13. A. E. Highley, *The First Sanctions Experiment: a Study of League
Procedures* (Geneva: Geneva Research Centre, Special Studies 9/4,
1938) 125.
14. See J. Joffe, 'Mixing Money and Politics: Dollars and Detente',
in A. S. Becker (ed.) *Economic Relations with the USSR* (Lexington,
Massachusetts: D. C. Heath, 1983) 17.
15. *Note Verbale* reproduced in *Europe: Documents* N. 1216 (Luxembourg: Agence Internationale d'Information Pour la Presse,
12 August 1982).
16. Ibid.
17. Augustin Hamon's phrase is quoted by D. Mitrany, *The Problem
of International Sanctions* (London: Oxford University Press, 1925)
39.
18. See Morley Morris, 'The United States and the Global Economic
Blockade of Cuba: a study in political pressures on America's
allies', *Canadian Journal of Political Science*, vol. 17, 1 (March 1984)
25–48.
19. Ibid., 33–4.
20. Ibid.
21. See A. E. Highley, loc. cit. in n. 13 above.
22. Lester B. Pearson, later Prime Minister of Canada, described the
work of the Committee of Eighteen of which he was a member as
a 'mockery ... used ... to sabotage and not enforce sanctions',

'Forty Years On: Reflections on our Foreign Policy', *International Journal*, vol. 22, 3 (1967) 359.

23. The Commonwealth Secretariat was established by Commonwealth Heads of Government in 1965.

24. The Committee's work is recorded in a series of annual reports. The first was submitted in December 1968 (SCOR, 23rd year, Special Supplement S/8954); the last in December 1979 (SCOR, 35th year, Special Supplement no. 2, vol. 1, 1980) in which it is recorded that the Committee ceased to exist on 21 December 1979, the date when sanctions were officially lifted by the Security Council.

25. See, for instance, the *Tenth Report of the Security Council Sanctions Committee* (SCOR, 33rd year, Special Supplement no. 2, vol. 1, S/ 12529, rev. I, para. 22.

26. P. J. Kuyper, *The Implementation of International Sanctions: the Netherlands and Rhodesia* (Alphen aan den Rijn: Sijthoff and Noordhoff, 1978). He writes of implementation 'as a legal mess which was largely ineffective', 206.

8 The Impact of Sanctions

1. See F. P. Walters, *A History of the League of Nations* (London: Oxford University Press, 1960) 650–1.

2. D. G. Clarke, 'Zimbabwe's International Economic Position and Aspects of Sanctions Removal', *Journal of Commonwealth and Comparative Politics*, vol. 18, 1 (March 1980) 28–54. He notes that 'international policy initiatives taken against the [Rhodesian] economy ... were in retrospect at least one step behind contingency initiatives of the Salisbury regime (29).

3. J. Galtung, 'On the Effects of International Economic Sanctions with examples from the case of Rhodesia', *World Politics*, vol. 19, 3 (April 1967) 409.

4. H. Strack, *Sanctions: the Case of Rhodesia* (Syracuse, New York: Syracuse University Press, 1978) 90.

5. *Note Verbale* reproduced in *Europe: Documents*, N. 1216 (Luxembourg: Agence Internationale d'Information Pour La Presse, 12 August 1982) 2. See too P. Geyelin in the *Guardian*, 30 October 1983, 'US Shot in the Foot a Soviet Shot in the Arm'.

6. M. J. Bonn, 'How Sanctions Failed', *Foreign Affairs*, vol. 15, 2 (1937) 360.

7. R. Renwick, *Economic Sanctions* (Cambridge, Massachusetts: Harvard Center for International Affairs, 1981) 50. See too C. C. Barnekov, 'Sanctions and the Rhodesian Economy', *Rhodesian Journal of Economics*, vol. 3, 1 (March 1969) 44–75.

8. *Economic Sanctions*, 39. An argument advanced by the US State Department in discussion of proposed US measures against Uganda was that a boycott of Uganda's main export, coffee, would be ineffectual because it could be rebagged elsewhere and given a non-Ugandan certificate of origin. See S. J. Fredman 'US Trade Sanctions against Uganda: Legality under International Law', *Law and Policy in International Business*, vol. 11, 3 (1979) 1160.

9. UN Sanctions Committee, *Tenth Report*, S/12529, rev. 1, vol. 1, 243.

10. See Chapter 7, n. 24.

11. See Chapter 4. There have been reports that the US embargo on Libyan oil has been undercut by loan and sale arrangements made by US oil companies operating in Libya. See the *Manchester Guardian Weekly*, 9 February 1986.

12. *Sanctions: the case of Rhodesia*, 98.

13. Cf. M. Edelman, *Politics as Symbolic Action* (Chicago: Markham Publishing Company, 1971) 76–80.

14. Cf. J. Galtung, loc. cit. in n. 3 above.

15. G. W. Baer, 'Sanctions and Security: the League of Nations and the Italian–Ethiopian War 1935–1936', *International Organization*, vol. 27, 2 (Spring 1973) 179.

16. See US 93rd Congress, 1st session. Data and analysis concerning the possibility of a US food embargo as a response to the present Arab oil boycott. *Report* prepared for the House Committee on Foreign Affairs by the Congressional Research Service (Washington, DC: 1973); US 94th Congress, *Oil Fields as Military Objectives: a Feasibility Study* (1974); R. W. Tucker, 'Oil: the Issue of American Intervention', *Commentary* January 1975, 21–31. An interview with Henry Kissinger, published in *Business Week*, 13 January 1975, is also relevant.

17. Victor Lavy, 'The Economic Embargo of Egypt by Arab States: myth and reality', *The Middle East Journal*, vol. 38, 3 (Summer 1984) 432.

18. See *The Front Line States: The Burden of the Liberation Struggle* (London: Commonwealth Secretariat, 1978).

19. See ibid. on Zambia and Tanzania's problems.

20. Ibid., 60.

21. Ibid., 60–1.

22. See Karen Lissakers, 'Money and Manipulation', *Foreign Policy*, No. 44 (Fall 1981) 107–26.

23. M. Goldman, 'The Evolution and Possible Direction of US Policy in East–West Trade' in A. S. Becker (ed.) *Economic Relations with the USSR* (Lexington, Massachusetts: D. C. Heath, 1983) 170. The freeze of Libyan government assets imposed by President

Reagan in January 1986 revived fears of a serious loss of confidence in security of foreign deposits.

24. Loc. cit. in n. 22, 120–1.

25. See *The Times*, 14 September 1982 ('Financial Sanctions Lifted by Britain').

9   The Case of South Africa

1. Mr Gavin Relly commented that in accepting the invitation of President Kaunda of Zambia to meet members of the ANC, he and fellow businessmen were not negotiating but engaging in a 'free and unrestricted exchange of views' which could help 'some degree of constructive understanding' to emerge. 'South Africa: a Time for Patriotism', *Manchester Guardian Weekly*, 6 October 1985, 15.

2. See *South African Digest* (Pretoria), 7 February 1986. Mr Botha also promised that all blacks living in South Africa would have their citizenship restored.

3. See, for instance, Leonard Thompson and Andrew Prior, *South African Politics* (New Haven, Connecticut: Yale University Press, 1982); Heribert Adam and Hermann Giliomee, *Ethnic Power Mobilized: Can South Africa Change?* (New Haven: Connecticut: Yale University Press, 1979); Arndt Spandau, *South Africa and the Western World* (Reutlingen: Verlag Harwalik KG, 1984); James Barber, *South Africa's Foreign Policy 1945–70* (London: Oxford University Press, 1973).

4. In particular the International University Exchange Fund published a 14-volume study *Economic Sanctions against South Africa* (Geneva: 1980); see too Adrian Leftwich (ed.) *South Africa: Economic Growth and Political Change* (London: Allison & Busby, 1974); James Barber, Jesmond Blumenfeld and Christopher R. Hill, *The West and South Africa* (London: Routledge & Kegan Paul for the Royal Institute of International Affairs, 1982). There are also many studies sponsored by the United Nations and non-governmental groups.

5. The major initiative for a sports boycott came from Commonwealth sources and in the 1977 Gleneagles Agreement, Commonwealth leaders agreed 'to withhold support for and to take every practical step to discourage contact or competition by their nationals with sporting organisations, teams or sportsmen from South Africa or from any other country where sports are organised on the basis of race, colour or ethnic origin'. A UN General Assembly Declaration against apartheid in sport was passed on 14 December 1977 (annex to res. 32/105 M), but EC members,

Australia, New Zealand and the United States abstained from voting. South Africa has been excluded from Olympic competition.

6. Text of the EC Code in 'The European Community and South Africa' (Brussels: Commission of the EC *Information* 166/77 E).

7. Reports on the implementation of the Sullivan Principles by firms signing them are published by the Arthur D. Little organisation.

8. 'South Africa: Strategy for Change', *Foreign Affairs*, 59, 2 (Winter 1980–81)   323–51.

9. Results of a survey conducted by Professor Lawrence Schlemmer at Natal University's Centre for Applied Social Sciences in 1984 suggested that 75 per cent of South African black workers were opposed to disinvestment. See report in the (Toronto) *Globe and Mail*, 24 September 1984.

10. See Deon Geldenhuys *What Do We Think? A survey of white opinion on foreign policy issues*. Braamfontein SA, The South African Institute of International Affairs (Occasional Paper) November 1982. See too comments by Mrs Helen Suzman MP, 'What the West Can Do', *Manchester Guardian Weekly*, 4 August 1985, emphasising her opposition to any steps that inhibit economic expansion and thereby deprive blacks of chances of increasing their economic leverage.

11. The resignation of Dr Van Zyl Slabbert, Leader of the Opposition, in February 1986 reflects the increasing frustration of whites as well as blacks.

12. See S. J. Ungar and Peter Vale, 'Why Constructive Engagement Failed', *Foreign Affairs*, 64, 2 (Winter 1985–6) 234–58; M. Clough, 'Beyond Constructive Engagement', *Foreign Policy*, No. 61 (Winter 1985–6) 3–24.

13. See J. H. Cooper, 'Economic Sanctions and the South African Economy', *International Affairs* Bulletin (SA Institute of International Affairs), 7, 2 (1983) 25–47.

14. South Africa Foundation, *1986 Information Digest* (Johannesburg, 1986). Trade in arms and oil is not disclosed.

15. UKSATA *British Trade With South Africa: a question of national interest* (London, 1982).

16. See South Africa Foundation, *1986 Information Digest*.

17. South Africa Chamber of Mines and Reserve Bank statistics.

18. J. H. Cooper, loc. cit. in n. 13, 31.

19. There are many studies of the west's mineral dependency. See particularly Library of Congress, Congressional Research Service, *Imports of Minerals from South Africa by the United States and the OECD countries* (Washington, DC: 1980); US House of Representatives, Committee on Interior and Insular Affairs, *Sub-Sahara Africa: its role in critical needs of the Western World* (Washington, DC: 1980).

20. See Report in the *Manchester Guardian Weekly*, 15 September 1985.
21. UKSATA *British Trade with South Africa*, 29.
22. The British Government initiated a small mineral stockpile in 1983. See report in the *Daily Telegraph*, 15 February 1983. The US maintains a stockpile of strategic minerals equal to about one year's supply.
23. See particularly M. Bailey and B. Rivers, *Oil Sanctions against South Africa*, UN: Centre Against Apartheid *Notes and Documents*, 12/78.
24. See Theo Malan, 'South Africa and Economic Sanctions', Supplement to *South African Digest*, 13 March 1981.
25. Ibid.
26. *The West and South Africa*, 57–8.
27. The US Council on Economic Priorities reported that six pension funds with combined assets exceeding $95 billion had joined the ranks of 'shareholder activists' in 1986. See report in the (Toronto) *Globe and Mail*, 27 February 1986.
28. UKSATA *British Trade with South Africa*, 13. There are no published official figures; UKSATA calculations are therefore estimates.
29. Ibid., 6.
30. A careful examination of the issues was provided by Merle Lipton. See 'British Investment in South Africa: Is Constructive Engagement Possible?' in Christian Concern for South Africa, *Investment in South Africa: the Options* (London, 1976).
31. See Economic Commission for Africa, *The Effect on Botswana, Lesotho and Swaziland of Sanctions Imposed against South Africa*, UN Doc. A/Conf. 107.1, 26 March 1981; see too J. Hanlon 'Conflict and Dependence in Southern Africa', *Third World Affairs* 1985 (London: Third World Foundation for Social and Economic Studies, 1985) 212–22.
32. See J. Barber and M. Spicer, 'Sanctions against South Africa: Options for the West', *International Affairs*, 55, 3 (July 1979) 400.
33. Statement quoted in the *Guardian*, 23 June 1981.
34. *South Africa 1984* (London: Routledge & Kegan Paul for the Royal Institute of International Affairs, 1985) 68. See too Clyde Ferguson and W. R. Cotter's '41 steps' in 'South Africa: What is to be done?', *Foreign Affairs*, 56, 2 (Winter 1977–8) 253–74.
35. *South Africa 1984*, 70.

10 Sanctions Revisited

1. The rejection by the Reagan Administration of the Law of the Sea Treaty in 1982, its decision to leave UNESCO and to withdraw US acceptance of the World Court's jurisdiction under

the Optional Clause in 1985, and a general scaling down of contributions to UN bodies in recent years all attest to this trend.

2. *Economic Statecraft* (Princeton, New Jersey: Princeton University Press, 1985) 205.

3. The cost factor is prominent in the list of 9 'Do's and Don'ts for governments contemplating sanctions provided by G. C. Hufbauer and J. Schott, *Economic Sanctions Reconsidered: History and Current Policy* (Washington, DC: Institute for International Economics, 1985) 91–2.

4. R. S. Olson, 'Economic Coercion in World Politics with a focus on North–South Relations', *World Politics*, 31, 4 (July 1979) 485.

5. S. Huntington, 'Trade, Technology and Leverage: Economic Diplomacy', *Foreign Policy*, 32 (Fall 1978) 63–80.

Index